START YOUR OWN COMPUTER BUSINESS

THE UNEMBELLISHED GUIDE

Morris Rosenthal

Please Read

The author has done his best to present accurate and up-to-date information in this book, but he cannot guarantee that the information is correct or will suit your particular situation. The book is sold with the understanding that the publisher and the author are not engaged in rendering legal, accounting or any other professional services. If expert assistance is required, the services of a competent professional should be sought.

Editor
Tracie Shea

Book Designer
Joe Gelles

Illustrator
Reva Rubenstein

Proof Reader
Franklyn Dailey Jr.

Published by Foner Books
www.fonerbooks.com
ISBN 0-9723801-0-8

TABLE OF CONTENTS

🛥 INTRODUCTION

Do you need your head examined? Probably, but I'm writing this book as a guide for those crazy folk who have already decided to start a computer business and are looking for some "been there, done that" advice. This guide is intended for the small start-up, not for somebody with deep pockets planning to launch a chain of retail stores. A lot of ink will be given to the hardware business, but software, services and training are where the small business stands the best chance of making a profit. The good news is that you can start a computer business with no money down, just like they say in furniture warehouse commercials. The bad news is that it's a really tough way to make a living, and most people who try don't just give up after a year or so of working for free, they LOSE MONEY. Why? Because running a successful computer business requires a true Jack or Jill of all trades. Sure, you recognize from the get-go that you need to be able to assemble, sell, and service PC's to enter the hardware business, though you might overestimate your abilities in one or more of these areas. The more commonly overlooked skills include: software troubleshooting, purchasing, inventory control (if you have inventory, you're out of control!), accounting, setting prices, customer relations, and time management. Perhaps the worst single pitfall in the computer hardware business is trying to compete on price. If all you have to offer is price, you're in for a nightmare.

Despite the warnings listed above, my basic "as is" advice is: If you're going to do it, jump in and do it. Start small (not that you have a choice) and let your skills and goals grow together. Don't get carried away with setting up the infrastructure for a "successful business" before you've even sold your first dozen PC's or billed 50 hours of training. Accounting and inventory software are great, but the paper checkbook register from the bank will give you plenty of insight into how you're doing in the initial stages. Don't invest money filling your basement with industrial racks or benches wired for networking. If you have a lot of cash on hand at the end of the year, there's plenty of time to stock up on toys after Christmas and still deduct them for the current tax year. Don't borrow money or mortgage your house. This book is about how to start a business on a shoe-string. You can learn more about business by trying to do it on the cheap than by throwing a lot of money around. In my experience, people who start out in the PC business with deep pockets are no more likely to succeed than those who start out having to scrape together money just to pay for parts. There are a lot of consultants out there who make a living "helping" people get started in business, and you're better off if you can't afford them. Being on a tight financial leash will force you to think about what you're doing.

⚓ YOUR FIRST SALE

You've sold your first PC to your mother's friend Doris, and then find out that whether you order it assembled or in pieces, there's not going to be any profit because you included Windows XP in the price but forgot to add in the cost. This drives you to ignore the top two tiers of distribution and go straight to the small importers with the aggressive pricing. You know the stuff is good because it says so on the fax. By using PriceWatch.com and going with the most aggressive pricing for each part, you figure you can scrape out a fifty dollar profit. You order an ATX case, keyboard and mouse from one place; a motherboard, CPU, RAM, hard drive and OEM Windows XP from a second place; and a floppy drive, video adapter, CD-ROM, modem, monitor and soundcard from a third place. Even the guy on the other coast promises you'll have the stuff within a week. The next day, the ATX case and power supply show up with the keyboard and mouse, and the UPS gal wants a check for $80. "What's this?" you say. "The parts cost was $71." The UPS gal explains that the shipping cost was $5 and the COD tag allowing you to pay with company check cost $4. You pay and go back to your spreadsheet to see where this is heading. Three days later, the motherboard, CPU, hard drive and Windows show up from the middle of the country by Fed-

X. You feel pretty good until you look at the invoice, which shows your credit card was billed for $355. Wait a minute, the parts total was $321. The bottom of the invoice shows a $29 item for 2nd day shipping, and another $5 for handling and insurance. You call the supplier, who reminds you that you wanted it by Thursday, and that he did tell you he was waiting for a shipment of RAM to arrive Tuesday morning. Well, at least you can give yourself credit that you bought the motherboard, CPU and RAM from a single vendor. Doing otherwise before your really know your vendors is pretty risky.

After assembling the parts that have arrived, you settle in to wait for the package from the other coast. It shows up after a week with a COD tag for exactly what you thought you were paying! Great! You pay, unpack the stuff to finish building your first PC and find the modem is missing. You read the invoice and see that the modem was "backordered" and the COD amount didn't include it. You run to the phone and call the vendor, who tells you, "Don't worry, it went out three days ago." "Call me next time before you backorder something on me," you yell at the voice. After you hang up, the voice says "Jerk." Three days later, the $29 modem shows up with a COD tag for $38. Hey, he did have to handle it separately, and the $4 for the COD is a constant. It's not the modem you ordered, but at this point, Doris is calling every day (she pre-paid), so you swallow a total of $81 ($9 + $34 + $29 +$9) in shipping, handling and insurance costs. You begin to see where ordering everything from one nearby vendor, preferably with net terms (non-COD) or a credit card, makes more sense than parting the thing out all over creation.

You put all the paperwork in a file folder labeled "Doris" and file it. This is really a critical step. Nobody will take defective stuff back without paperwork, unless you have a real good relationship and can get the salesman to look it up on their computer system for you. You finish putting the PC together, load Windows XP, and everything is great. You load all the driver CDs for the video, modem, and sound card (you forgot to include speakers in the price), and Windows XP now takes twice as long to boot. Par for the course. The monitor gives off an odor like burning plastic on an ocean breeze, but you figure that will clear up. You run Scan Disk a couple times, wonder what a 24 hour burn-in really means, and if you should spend a hundred dollars on some testing software. Unless you have money to burn, don't bother. Just leave the thing turned on over night and check that it still works in the morning. It's a decent test, and you're doing a lot more than most guys I've known.

You put the PC in the car, and drive it to the customer's home. If you were a mail-order business you could leave it on the doorstep, ring the doorbell and run, but you aren't. You take the PC out of the box and plug everything together. Your customer turns it on, the Microsoft flag appears, so you leave your homemade business card and go home relieved that you only lost around $31 selling your first PC. You use a hobby knife to cut up the boxes that Doris didn't want and you put them out for recycling day. The foam peanuts you save, believing that eventually they'll come in handy- good luck. The next morning the phone rings, your first tech support call. Doris bought an inkjet printer at Staples (they had it cheaper than any price you could find) and it doesn't work – Staples tells her it sounds like a computer problem. You warn your mother's dearest and oldest friend that if it's not a computer problem, you'll have to charge her your $50 field service rate, and she agrees. You arrive at her house, and immediately see that she's trying to use old typewriter paper in the printer and the paper isn't heavy enough for the feeder, producing all sorts of jams and "printer not ready or not connected" errors. Since you only spend two minutes in the house and it's such a silly problem, you can't bring yourself to charge her.

Being the clever sort, you cut a deal with your local Internet Service Provider (ISP) where they promise to pay you $100 at the end of the year for each new customer you deliver to them. You call your customer, talk her out of going with AOL or Compuserve, which her son in Dallas has told her to get, and you drive out and create a dial-up-networking connection to her new ISP. You set her up with Internet Explorer and Outlook Express, spend two or three hours teaching her how to use e-mail and buy junk on E-Bay. Then you go home satisfied that you're now making the $35 to $50 an hour you always knew you were worth, even if you won't get it for twelve months.

Unfortunately, when her son visits for Christmas, he convinces her that she can save big bucks by signing a multi-year deal with a national provider, and your $100 miraculously vanishes. Adding insult to injury, the day after New Year's she calls you to say the modem isn't working anymore. On hearing that she has moved to AOL, you spend a half-hour on the phone angrily explaining that it's probably a software problem, and that you'll have to charge that elusive $50 field rate if you come out. She agrees, and you show up to find that the modem really did die.

You go home, pull out the "Doris" folder, call the vendor, who gives you an RMA (Return Merchandise Authorization) number and tells you he'll ship a replacement. You breathe a sigh of relief that the vendor is still in business, since you haven't talked to him in three months, and then send off the modem. After a week, you call, and he explains that he has to ship it back to his supplier, but they turn stuff around really fast, and you should have the replacement within two weeks. You give up and call your local importer and buy another $29 modem, paying with a credit card. It comes the next day and you install it. Doris is pretty upset at having been offline for a week, and suggests that maybe you've bitten off more than you can chew in "your little computer business." Two months later, her original modem arrives in a beat up package from some place you never heard of with a note saying they tested it fully and it worked for them. You put it in your own PC to test it and immediately smell smoke. Welcome to the PC business.

BUSINESS OR HOBBY?

To B, or not to B

Many people who plan to start a computer business first became involved with computers as a hobby. Perhaps you were the only person in your office or classroom who could get the network printer to work, or you discovered the joys of hardware repair through cleaning the lint off some mouse rollers. Maybe you arrived here through the software side, helping friends and family get online with e-mail and web surfing. The one thing you can be sure of is that there's a big difference between having a hobby and running a business. For the purpose of this book, we'll differentiate between a business and a hobby as follows: A business makes money, a hobby costs money. For those folks out there who are making money at what they call their "hobby," I have good news, you're already running a successful business. If any of you are currently losing money in what you intended to be a business, I hope that at least you're getting some entertainment value for your dollar. In this chapter we will survey some of the decisions you need to make before you start a business and the factors that play into them. All of the subjects touched on here will be treated in more detail in later.

The main paradox of being in business is that when you sell something, you own it forever. If you're a tough guy, forever only lasts until the warranty expires, but saying "no" can require some real guts. Whether you are selling hardware, software or services, you are always accepting some degree of responsibility where before you had none. If nothing else, you should keep it in mind when you're setting your prices. You'll find the experience to be similar to religious laws governing ritual impurity. The only way to get clean involves taking a bath. Anything you touch will be forever after linked to your face and phone number, and the best you can hope for is that the time will be billable.

How Much Money do You Need?

When you set out to support yourself (not to mention any spouse and kiddies) through starting a new business, the very first question you must answer for yourself is, "How much money do I need to take home each week?" If you're lucky enough not to have any bills or to have somebody to pay them for you, skip this paragraph. The question addresses weekly take home, not a yearly figure, and there are at least three good reasons for looking at income this way. First, it should immediately make it clear to you how long you can spend trying to establish your business. If you need to bring home $500 a week to keep up with the bills, and you have $5000 you want to gamble on starting a business, things look pretty grim. It quickly becomes apparent that even if you could set up a business without spending a dime, you don't have very long to get up to speed earning an after tax profit of $500 a week. The second reason to start looking at income as a weekly figure is that small computer businesses rarely have steady income. The potential for a profit of $8,000 in December won't help much if your car or house is being auctioned off by the bank in October. The third reason for looking at income from a weekly perspective is that it should bring home the amount of business you'll need to do in an average week.

Another common scenario for launching people into business is a windfall, such as severance pay, an inheritance, or a lump sum distribution from a savings plan. I've never known anybody who had any luck starting a business just because they got a financial head start. As important as the money is, it's your professional and business skills that will make the difference between success and failure. The amount of money you start with mainly impacts the amount of money you can lose if it doesn't work out. It can even be a negative, because sometimes banks or vendors will grant you credit based on your cash value, allowing you to lose even more than you started with. The only instance where I've seen free money help out is in the case of unemployment benefits, which are distributed slowly, and can help a person keep their head above water while having the opportunity to work full time at starting something new.

The worst financial mistake you can make is underestimating the amount of money you need to keep up with the lifestyle to which you're accustomed. The broader philosophical question of how much money do you need to be happy, or at least not to become desperate, is worth spending a few words on. Some people are very good at living on pennies, and may actually enjoy it. Others will never buy something in one store if they can pay more across the street. In my personal experience, there is very little mobility between these two groups, and the habits are probably formed in childhood. If you consider eating out a couple times a week a necessity rather than a lark, you aren't cut out for living on a shoestring. That doesn't mean you can't make it in the computer business, it's just to warn you to add a couple points to your selling margins. If you consider takeout and a video on Friday evening a cheap night, you probably fall in the middle of the curve, but you'll be competing with some people who work every Friday night and don't own a VCR.

Accepting Ultimate Responsibility

The biggest difference between running a business and hobby is that in a business, failure is unacceptable. When you're fixing computers for friends and family for free and you run into a problem you can't solve, you might get embarrassed, but hopefully you won't get sued. When you're doing it as a business, charging for your time or supporting hardware and services you've previously sold and guaranteed, you're on the hook. It's also a big adjustment to go from working as a technician for an established business with a boss you can call if things go wrong, to being the sole individual responsible. The first time you go out to do a simple memory upgrade on somebody's network server and you get a "Hard Drive Failure" when you power it back up, your stomach will sink into your sneakers. It's the wrong time to start asking when they did their last backup. I've been out on many such service calls, either for myself or in support of other independents I've worked with, and as the "hardware guy", it's been up to me to make it right. It's really takes some time to get used to the fact that when it comes to commodity hardware, there is nobody you can call. You are the end of the line. Configuration problems with new, branded hardware and software are much easier to deal with because of tech support at these companies, usually free for licensed users.

Just a few months before I started writing this book, I got stuck redoing 20 hours of software development for a customer whose hard drive failed when their air conditioning went down, and whose last good backup was a month old. It took around ten hours just to get to the point where that old backup tape would restore, and believe me, I was sweating bullets worrying I'd have to go all the way back to the last CD backup I'd made with my own equipment the previous summer. In this case, the customer offered to pay for my time for both the repairs and the rework, but because I had set up the original tape backup system and had failed to make sure that the incremental back-ups were still working each week, I took it as my responsibility. Pride has its costs. I did try sending out the hard drive to a data recovery outfit, since my memory isn't what it once was and I really wasn't enthusiastic rewriting the code from scratch, but it was a head crash and nothing could be salvaged.

Earn While You Learn

If part of your plan is to open a retail storefront, then you're looking at starting right in at 60+ hours a week. If you're planning on working out of the home, you may be able to start the business on a part-time footing. This is particularly well suited to students, people who are currently supporting themselves wholly or partially through another part-time job, and people who have an income from another business that doesn't require all of their time. The safest thing you can go into business selling is your time. If you can pick up part-time work doing training or software development, your business will see an immediate net profit. The trick is not plowing all the money from the "winning" side of your business into an unproven, "losing" side. It's a tempting strategy to minimize your tax load by re-investing your profits, but I've seen hundreds of thousands of dollars disappear into the black hole of new product and services development based on off-the-shelf products. In the end, you'll have nothing to show for it but some certificates on the wall and memories of indigestion from eating the luncheon at their vendors convention.

Starting out as a low-key, part-time operation will give you plenty of time to experiment with ways to attract customers, but if you jump into making the computer business your sole occupation, you'd better be good at sales. If you build a better PC, nobody is going to beat a path to your door; you need to go out and sell it. We'll talk about advertising and other sales techniques in more detail later, but the two most important weapons in the sales arsenal are word-of-mouth and cold calling. Word of mouth remains the best way to increase your customer base, but you have to find those initial mouths on your own. A friend of mine who worked for a while as an insurance salesman used to say, "The easiest sales pitch to blow off is a mailing, and the next easiest is a phone call. If you really want to get somebody to listen, you've got to show up in person." Showing up in person to sell your goods and services to people who don't know you from Adam is the cold call. Many people will find that they can't even stand the rejection of the lightweight version of the cold call, which is phoning first to try to get an appointment. If you've never tried getting a job somewhere that wasn't advertising for help, you may be in for trouble before you even start. The secret to good word of mouth is good service, and the worst thing you can ever do to hurt your image is to over-promise. If a customer wants more than you can deliver, either don't make the sale or gamble on investing the time in pre-sale customer education to bring them around to realistic expectations.

Managing Money

A final question to ask yourself before you set out on the path to self-employment is, "Do you balance your checkbook?" Anybody who can do addition and subtraction has the ability to balance a checkbook, but some people prefer to live in ignorance. Maybe if you're selling illegal drugs or pumping oil out of the ground, you can watch the thousands and let the smaller amounts take care of themselves. In the computer business, the small amounts spent on shipping can make all the difference between success and failure, and indeed many mail order businesses count on their shipping and handling mark-up for a large proportion of their profits. If you want to be in business for yourself, you need to handle money for yourself. You can outsource tax preparation and bookkeeping, but you can't outsource decision making and budgeting, which is what balancing your checkbook is all about. We mentioned earlier that you're now the end of the line when you're out doing a service call. It's equally important to realize that you're now the end of the line on purchasing decisions. Bad purchasing will put you out of business even faster than bad service. As long as we're on the subject of money, I would discourage you from starting a business if you are in the habit of carrying a balance on your credit card. The ability to manage scarce financial resources is an absolute requirement in small business, and if you are already dipping into credit card financing just to manage your personal expenses, you don't stand much of a chance.

All of these questions and answers should be used to formulate a business plan. We aren't talking about a business plan to bring to a bank. They aren't going to give you any money anyway. The important thing is to get the basic facts down on paper so you don't end up pulling the wool over your own eyes.

Start with all of your current, pre-business expenses, none of which will go away just because you start working for yourself. This dollar figure needs to be included in the plan as your salary, which you need to pay yourself whether you're making a profit or not. If you can live on air, you're that much ahead of the game, but be realistic. Identify your target markets (everyone doesn't count) and do a little market research. Go ask your potential customers where they are currently buying their computers and services, and why they chose these vendors. Estimate how many hours of service you'll be able to sell and divide by two, or by four if you're an optimist. Rough out the expenses of a retail location and stock if that's your goal. Put down every last expense you can think of, and be sure that you're still missing plenty. The point of this business plan is to open your eyes and help you differentiate between the probable and the merely possible. The Service Corps Of Retired Executives (SCORE) offers free counseling to budding entrepreneurs across the country (toll free 1-800-634-0245 or www.score.org. SCORE is a non-profit group with ties to the SmallBusiness Administration (SBA), and they are particularly good at helping with business plans and early stage strategizing.

🚢 BUYING AND SELLING

Buying Computer Hardware

There are three basic places you can go to buy computer parts and software, and none of them involve going directly to the manufacturer. The top tier of distributors, Ingram Micro, Tech Data, Merisel and the like, sell everything you could ever want, but on basic clone computer hardware, they can't compete on price. These top distributors will get you going pretty quick on financing, and offer something called "floor planning" to finance purchases for retail operations, but since we aren't talking about opening a shop in prime Main Street space just yet, leave that thought on the back-burner. The main items you're likely to want from the big distributors early on include software (except operating systems, which you'll buy in OEM versions with the PC parts), printers and other brand name peripherals that your customers insist on.

The second source for computer parts are the importers/ OEMs. Original Equipment Manufacturers (OEMs) in the PC business generally mean people who import or buy direct from domestic manufacturers and put together privately branded PCs. You might think this takes all the fun out of it for you, but there are myriad advantages. First of all, by sticking with OEMs who have been in business at least five years or so, there'll be a good chance the phone won't be disconnected when you call the next week. Second, this is all they do for a business, while your real business is being a small business. Third, it greatly simplifies the warranty and defective merchandise return process if you get whole PCs from one place, rather than scattering your parts orders across a half dozen low-ball vendors each week. Lastly, since OEMs want to sell computers in large numbers, if you stumble into a big sale before you have the organization or financing to handle it, you can cut a deal where they deliver to your customer and even send the bill. You show up and take the PCs out of the boxes, and you earn a handsome commission.

Finally there are the nickel-dime (meaning five million to ten million dollar annual revenue) importers and OEM wanna-be's. These are the outfits that will have the best pricing on stuff that you don't exactly want, but that you can make a profit selling. For a machine here and there, the risk isn't that great, though I tend to pay more attention to the brands of the actual components when buying them from folks who probably won't be around forever. It's best to settle quickly on one or two of these outfits, at least one of which is close enough for UPS ground to show up the next day. Inventory is a killer in the PC business, so being able to get stuff quickly without paying extra for overnight or second day shipping is a big plus. The biggest problem you'll encounter in dealing with these smaller operations is that due to their relatively low volume, you'll often end up buying a system that they've never built with exactly those parts before. When it doesn't work, they'll be happy to start swapping parts (with shipping costs and delays), but you're the one who will have to explain to your customer why the troubleshooting process seems so random.

How do you get in touch with these vendors, and should you invest time filling out paperwork for strategic alliances with everybody who is willing? It is definitely worth while to sign up with Ingram and Tech Data and jump through whatever hoops they request. These distributors will soon grant you company credit, which helps you establish credit with other vendors down the line. You should also pick one big name, like IBM or HP, that you can obtain through these distributors, and fill out the paperwork for whatever reseller program they happen to be pushing that month. This doesn't mean you can expect to open any doors selling brand-name hardware, but if you happen upon a business customer who likes you for your prompt and friendly service, you'll regret it if you aren't in a position to make the easy sale. The mid-tier OEMs and small importers will start contacting you, by phone or fax, as soon as you establish a buying persona in the trade. You can get a jump on being found by wholesalers by searching PriceWatch.com or calling the 800 numbers in PC magazines and asking if they have a wholesale operation in addition to mail-order retail. In the end, it takes a while to get established with vendors you can trust, and the smaller the number of suppliers you deal with, the better off you are. One resource I consider well worth the subscription cost is The Resellers Source Kit at www.rs-kit.com. The annual subscription price is $80 (you can buy a single issue for half that) and it includes over 1,500 true wholesalers, overgrown resellers, and liquidators, splendidly organized and updated every month.

This brings up an interesting exception to the "don't spend anything" rule of thumb that applies to doing business on a shoestring. If you can buy some reasonable service or information that may be critically important to the success of your business, AND it wouldn't build your useful skill base by doing this work yourself, spend the money. While learning more about taxes or marketing makes you a more valuable entrepreneur, spending hundreds of hours on the phone trying to build a database of potential vendors is a waste of time. Better to hang onto your day job one extra day and use the pay to get a one month jump on starting your own business.

The only real way to lower your cost on computer parts beyond the established pricing of your vendors is to bargain with them. Even the top tier distributors give their salespeople some flexibility on pricing. A fellow I used to work with would call up either Ingram or Tech Data and get a price on an item. Then he'd knock off $5 and call the other saying, "I got a price from your competitor of $X". It usually worked, though you need to have a certain type of personality to do that day in and day out. The OEMs and smaller importers are also flexible on price, but you won't find out without pushing them. There is a risk in pushing too hard, however, in that you'll never develop a good relationship with the salesperson, who needs to earn a living also. Salespeople are instrumental in expediting returns, rush shipments, and even getting you access to tech support. It's a hard balance to strike, but I usually come down on the side of establishing a good relationship and adjusting selling prices to compensate.

The fool's gold of purchasing is buying quantity to get lower pricing. This may work in some retail businesses, but not with computers. The shelf life for items like hard drives and memory is similar to that of fresh produce in the super market. Computer parts suffer from a type of spoilage I would characterize as premature obsolescence. New hardware is being released every month, and even if your customers don't push you for the latest thing, the emergence of new products causes the prices of the older products to fall as vendors who bought in quantity to get discounts try to unload them. The sole exception to this rule is the occasional shortages that show up in the spot market, particularly for memory, but these are entirely unpredictable and usually of a short duration. In summary, you should never buy more parts then you need to fill an order, though you might pop for some spare parts on very large orders to avoid delays.

The owner of an outfit I was working for around 15 years ago wanted to get good pricing by buying wholesale from Asia, so he ordered the minimum number of retail boxed mice he could to deal direct with the manufacturer. At the time, mice were fairly expensive, and since he had to buy over a thousand, this tied up several tens of thousands of dollars. Since we didn't really have an established retail channel and weren't selling anywhere near enough PCs to recover this investment in a reasonable amount of time, we decided to try one of the large indoor computer fairs that used to be quite common. All day Sunday, a couple of us stood behind a six foot table selling these mice for $35, which was the cheapest price at the show. I made the mistake of joking with one customer, who asked where we had obtained them so cheap, that they had fallen off a truck. Lost that sale, but we sold all the mice we brought, recovering the capital invested for more important purposes.

When you purchase parts from out-of-state, which you commonly will do unless you live in California or the Far East, you won't be charged sales tax. However, when you purchase parts within the state where your business is run, you'll need to register with the state and get a reseller tax ID. Actually, many out of state vendors will also require your reseller tax ID, either because they have an office in your state or because they require it from everybody. There are still four or five states left in America with no sales tax, for whom this doesn't apply. Vendors in your state may require a photocopy or fax of this certificate to drop the sales tax from your purchases. If you wonder why your state is being so generous and waiving sales tax on your purchase, it's because when you sell merchandise within the state, you'll be required to charge sales tax and turn it over to the state (and sometimes city), and they get very nasty if you forget. An excellent starting point for determining the requirements of your state is the Small Business Administration (SBA), a federal agency that promotes the development of small businesses with educational programs and loan guarantees www.sba.gov/starting.

Buying Software and Books

Almost all of the PCs you sell, unless you have geeky clientele, will require a Microsoft operating system. Whether you are buying bare-bones PCs or assembling them from scratch, you'll need to purchase OEM Windows right along with your other components. It's not worth going direct with Microsoft unless you sell a huge number of systems. Your suppliers will also be able to get you OEM versions of the big Microsoft applications, like Office. When it comes to buying software for CD burners and other specialty hardware, the best source is usually the vendor you're buying the hardware from. If you do buy OEM software for burning CDs or doing Optical Character Recognition (OCR) on scanned images, make sure that it is the full version or that it covers your specific hardware.

Games software and educational CD's are available for incredibly cheap prices from web merchants in bulk, but most of it is stuff you'll never resell. The top tier distributors carry the most popular games in shrink wrapped boxes, and you can return them if they don't sell within a reasonable amount of time. I've never looked into going direct with a games manufacturer, though I probably would if I was currently in retail. The prime concern when stocking games software is that the distributor not be some fly-by-night outfit, because you don't want to end up owning the software you can't sell.

If you have a retail shop, one of the most profitable items you could end up selling is computer books. It's rarely worthwhile for a small store to directly approach a publisher for books, so most stores obtain books through distribution. The biggest book distributors in the US are Ingram Books (www.ingrambookgroup.com) and Baker&Taylor (www.btol.com), but there's an excellent third option specifically for computer books. Koen Distribution (www.koen.com) offers two special programs for retail locations, their In-Store Service and their EZ program.

With the In-Store Service program a Koen representative will come to your store every 8 weeks to pull returns, arrange the section, and spot-check your inventory to ensure you have the proper titles. You'll receive around 40 new titles per month on Net-30 terms, with a 2% discount for early payment. Accounts with the In-Store Service program usually stock 200 books or more.

The EZ program features two lists, the EZ-50 and the EZ-100, from which smaller stores stock books. There's a little more paperwork and overhead involved, since a there are no regular visits from a Koen representative to keep track of things for you. Both the EZ and the In-Store Service feature penalty free returns and sell you all books at a 43% discount, so you earn over $10 on a $25 book. Koen will notify you of any titles that go out-of-print, so you can return them in time, and they also provide book reviews. If you're just starting to build retail traffic and you don't have a lot of money, the lower stocking requirement of the EZ program will be the way to go. However, if you do have some spare capital, the profit margin is excellent and the more books you stock, the more you're likely to sell. Having a strong book section may also help pull customers into your store.

Financing Purchases

It may seem silly to start talking about different types of money, but the truth is, all dollars are not created equal. When it comes to financing your purchases, there are three possible currencies: real money (cash), credit and debt. Cash means money that you have in the bank, not greenbacks that you carry in your pocket. You can write checks or do wire transfers to buy merchandise with money you have in the bank, and you won't receive any bills later on. The money was real, the purchase was real, end of story.

The difference between credit and debt is a little more subtle. By credit financing, we aren't talking about using your credit card, that's actually debt. Credit is when vendors will send you merchandise on "terms" other than COD (Cash on Delivery). Some vendors, such as OEMs, may grant you "Net-30" terms, meaning you have 30 days to pay their invoice. You won't get these terms immediately; you have to do some business with them to gain their confidence. While these OEMs will charge you a stiff interest rate if you go over 30 days, they aren't in the banking business so they'd rather be paid on time. If you can get your customers to pay you within 30 days, it means that you can sell large dollar amounts of hardware that you could never have financed with cash. Importers rarely grant credit since their business is built on turning over their cash as frequently as possible. Companies like Ingram and Tech Data will quickly give you a real line of credit (based in part on your personal credit worthiness and guarantee), but initially the amount will be rather small. A bank will normally only give a new small business a line of credit based on personal assets, such as your home, so it's not worth wasting your time pursuing this your first year in business.

The third type of debt is when you borrow from Peter to pay Paul, and Peter charges you 15% or more for the privilege. In other words, if your vendors will only sell to you COD, and you use your credit card to pay them, you are financing your business through debt.

Leasing is standard only for items you don't need and shouldn't be buying anyway, like cars and office equipment, which is why salespeople for these items can always offer you lease terms.

There is one more method of paying for merchandise, after the sale, that I'm going to tell you about just so you can avoid it. Companies that give you financing based on invoices for merchandise you have already delivered to customers, called "Factors," are essentially loan sharks. Basically, they purchase your accounts receivable (the money you bill your customers) at a discount, and charge you interest on the remaining amount until your customer pays. For example, if you've sold $10,000 of merchandise to a customer who is a slow pay, a factor would charge you something like 5% for making the deal plus a first months interest of 1.5%, so the actual sum of money you would receive from the factor is around $9,350. If your customer is slow on paying, you could owe the factor additional 1.5% chunks on the original $10,000. Even if your customer pays on time, you've given up a quarter of your profit, just to get back the use of your money. If you sold the merchandise cheaper than you should have, which is often the case, you could end up making nothing on the sale, and still be responsible for service down the road.

Establishing Credentials

How do you establish credentials and why should anybody trust you? Well, it turns out that the best way to convince somebody that you're a computer expert is to show up and do something for them. Outside of the human resources departments of bland companies, nobody knows or cares what an A+ certified technician or a certified Microsoft or Novell engineer is. When you're in business for yourself, people will buy PCs from you because you show up and sell them. Nobody will ask you where you learned to put them together (or to buy them cheap), anymore than you ask the person who comes and installs the phone lines where they learned to do it. It's enough that they show up. In small business, your credentials are your honest face, your word of mouth, your Yellow Pages listing, your website, and your storefront if you have one. You're going to need all the cash you can get your hands on. Don't waste it on pieces of paper that nobody will read to frame and stick on the wall. That's a game for the people who want to be somebody else's employee.

One of your biggest selling points will be your promise of prompt and friendly service. In order to compete with the national mail-order outfits like Dell and Gateway who offer onsite warranty service, you'll have to do the same. The problem here should be immediately apparent. If you spend money to rent a retail space, it better be open during retail hours. But how can you be out doing service calls during the hours any business customers will insist on while keeping your store open?

The answer is, you can't, unless you have a partner or an employee. If you do have a retail location, you can try getting a part-time student for after school hours and try to schedule all your service calls in the afternoon, but it will cost you some standing with business customers who want it fixed now. Unless you can get such a good deal on a space that you can afford to NOT be open all the time, signing a lease means giving up on being a one person shop.

You can't expect to compete on price with boxed systems from Best Buy or Walmart. You could probably find some super cheap junk from importers that would let you make the sale without losing money, but the first time the phone rings for warranty service, you're out of pocket. You need to educate the customer about the difference between you and the big chain stores, and also the difference between their hardware and the hardware you're selling. Don't quote the closest system you can manage, quote something better. For $50 more in cost you can double the size of the hard drive or the RAM, or replace the CD with a CDR. Make sure you give the customer a reason to choose your system by giving them more, without regard to the price. Hopefully your customers will feel they're worth it.

Setting Prices

Establishing pricing comes after lining up vendors for a reason: You can't set your prices until you know how much you'll be paying for parts. If you listen to PC distributors, you'll hear them blowing a lot of smoke about selling on margins under 5% and making a living. What they're talking about is a PROFIT of 5%, figuring most costs up front. You have no way of knowing your costs up front, as you aren't even in business yet. To make a living selling and servicing PC hardware in the

$100,000 to $1,000,000 a year range, I can offer a couple rules of thumb based on experience. If you are working out of your house, and you are very disciplined about charging for extras (that $50/hr+ field rate we keep mentioning), you never want to sell anything under 15 points. A 15 point margin isn't the same as "15% of", but a divisor. Take the real cost of the item you are selling, including shipping cost, and divide it by 0.85 (the 15 points comes from 1.00 - 0.15 = 0.85). This gives you a pre-tax sales price of $824 for a $700 investment in parts. If you have already jumped into a retail operation with a leased space and a helper of some sort, a more realistic margin is around 20 points (divide by 0.80) meaning that $700 PC must be sold for $875. These numbers are based on experience! If you can't at least reach these margins, you're running a money losing hobby, not a business. If you get involved with selling PCs for under $500 or $600, you better add another 5 points to the margins given above. Part of the profit you are trying to achieve is really a reserve against warranty service, and cheap PCs have at least as many problems and service calls associated with them as their more expensive brethren.

To drive the point home, let's say your town was starving for a new computer business, and you have no trouble doing $200,000 in hardware business your first year, exclusive of sales taxes. Some of your customers want the cheapest PC they can get, others buy screaming game machines, and your average selling price is $1000. This means you are delivering an average of four computers a week out of your small retail establishment and at a 20 point margin, your average cost is $800 per machine (800 / 0.8 = 1000). On hardware and software, your $200,000 in gross sales has brought you a gross profit of $40,000. Your triple net rent for 1000 sq ft in Anysmalltown, USA, along with all office expenses and insurance comes to

$1,000 per month, or $12,000 for the year (you got a great deal, by the way). Your gross profit is now down to $28,000. If you had operated out of your house at a 15 point margin, your gross profit would have been $30,000, and allowing $2000 for business phone and similar office expenses, you end up at the same $28,000 for the year. This $28,000 does not include your mistakes, your car expenses, or any office equipment you felt you had to buy. Sure, you can write-off expenses, and for grins, we'll allow you $8000 worth, but that doesn't mean as much as you think in the end. Assuming you are functioning as a sole proprietor, you'll end up owing self-employment tax on $20,000, which amounts to about $3000 off the top, and you'll probably owe some State and Federal income tax, depending on your personal situation (kids, mortgage, etc.). The $8000 dollars in deductions we gave you were backed by real expenses so it's not money you have anymore; you did put miles on the car, buy a laser printer and a $500 ad in the local paper. On your $200,000 in sales, you're left with a little less than $17,000 to divide between you and the income tax man.

OK, you would have been happy with $34,000, but could you have done the over $400,000 in hardware business to get it? At our average selling price, you need to sell, deliver and service eight PCs a week. In order to sell $400,000 of product with a gross cost of over $300,000, you'll need a minimum of $25,000 in cash and credit available each month, and not all of your customers will pay within 30 days. Cash flow management means having the money or credit available to buy stuff to make more money, and it is a critical skill as you try to grow your business. Remember, you may have no sales all summer, then do well in October and November, tying up all your money. December rolls around, you have $100,000 of potential Christmas sales and no credit left to buy hardware until your invoices get paid! The point is, it's not so easy to just sell more to make more money.

Nobody wants to work for less than $17,000 a year (and no health insurance or benefits), so you're wondering if there's something wrong with our model. Well, we left out that high margin income you can expect to earn selling by your time once you're established as a local computer expert. This includes repairing PCs for people who bought them elsewhere; doing upgrades, where your labor cost is an expected line item; field service; software support; and training if you are so inclined. Well dressed techs from big companies may charge over $100 an hour for field service. When you're starting out, you're probably better off keeping your rates down in the $75 - $50/hr for field service and $50 - $35/hr for shop work, and getting the business. Now we see that if you can sell ten or fifteen hours of your time each week, you'll be adding over $25,000 a year in gross income. That's more than $20,000 after self-employment tax and extra expenses, getting your annual income back up into the high thirties. All this assumes that you're actually working the sixty or more hours a week that it will take to get there. Remember, most who try this business fail, because they never actually make these numbers. They don't charge enough for the machines they sell and they try to increase business by adding salaried staff who only increase the losses by selling more stuff at low margins.

The worst thing you can do is try to win customers on price. If you beat yourself up on price before you even try selling to customers, you're never going to make a living wage. Don't get stuck promising long warranties (over a year) that some OEMs will offer you. Those OEMs will be out of business long before that 3 year or 5 year warranty expires, and if you're still in business, you'll get stuck footing the bill. When you're a small business, the main thing you have to sell is YOU. Whether or not you feel in your heart that you're better than the competition, this is what you have to sell your customers on.

The Quantity Discount Trap

The quantity discount trap applies to selling just as much as buying. If somebody comes to you and wants to buy twenty PCs with the associated network installation and extras to set up a classroom or an office, by all means, get quantity pricing from your vendors and pass the savings along to the customer. After all, a juicy network installation is highly profitable if you do the work yourself (most companies charge at least $175 per drop, which means per system installed). Sounds great, huh? The danger with granting discounts for quantity purchases is that the "quantity" part of the purchase may never materialize. The trap plays out something like this: A new potential customer, usually another small business who sells some PC based product like point-of-sale systems or doctor's office software, will come to you with a tempting deal. "I need to buy two or three PCs a week," the customer will say, "But I don't want to be in the PC business myself and I'm tired of dealing with these mail-order outfits. Here's an invoice for a PC I just bought. If you can meet their price, you have my business."

Now, the invoice this potential customer shows you is for a slightly obsolete model that the mail-order vendor was unloading cheap, but you figure you can get quantity pricing from the OEM you're on good terms with and clear $100 a unit. WRONG THINKING. First of all, customers like this will never sign a contract to buy a large quantity of PCs from you, so the only guarantee you have that this really is a quantity sale is their say-so. Next, you won't be able to get quantity discounts from your vendors for product shipped over a period of time unless you sign a commitment to take delivery of it all, and you better not. Furthermore, the customer who is looking for the cheapest possible PC will never stop looking, so you can't assume that as parts prices drop you'll be able to make up the money you didn't make up front. Lastly, you should never break your pricing discipline for somebody who is only buying one unit at a time. Selling cheap PCs is a terrible business to be in, because your investment in time is identical up front to selling more expensive PCs, but you only make a fraction of the profit, even if you maintain your selling margins. Cheap PCs are also more likely to create a service headache as they'll be built with whatever junk some supplier had left over, but you'll have to offer the same warranty you offer on higher priced units. For a hands-off bid where you are essentially acting as a sales representative, you can afford to lower your margins, but for hardware that you have to finance and service, you can't play with your pricing model every time a promising deal walks in the door.

Competitive bids for schools and other public institutions are another matter. It's worth bidding on a few of these just to find out about the local competition and how they price the bids. However, most bids are written to specify certain hardware, vendors with multiple years in business or sales of similar sizes, and other factors that will exclude you from competing in your early years. The only way around this is to bid them as a representative for one of the OEMs or distributors we mentioned previously. Top tier distributors and large OEMs have "bid desks," salespeople who specialize in preparing pricing for government bids. They can meet all of the bid requirements except for having a local office, which is where you come in. Be aware, however, that many bids are rigged and aren't worth get-

B-School Follies

ting too excited about. Purchasing managers often have sweet-heart relationships with certain vendors and write bid RFPs (Request for Proposals) specifically for that vendor. Some state and local governments also have "blanket contracts" which go out for bid once a year or less. Vendors who get on these blankets can then sell to cities and schools directly, bypassing the competitive bid process. It's worth a visit to your local state purchasing office to ask about blanket contracts, and to bid on these whenever they come up. State university systems may also issue blanket contracts on an annual or biannual basis. A position on any blanket contract can make your whole business, but don't confuse a license to sell with a license to make money. You still have to compete with other vendors on the blanket, and many government entities are slow pays, tying up your money up for months.

Advertising vs. Selling

Selling is an art. When I started out as an engineer, I used to look down on salesmen as a sort of lower form of life who made a living conning people into buying junk they didn't need. Well, it turns out that capitalism and apple pie are based on salesmanship, without which the whole economy would return to the barter system. It's possible to make a living without being a good salesperson, though it will take extra servings of luck and phenomenal word of mouth. It's really worth the old school try to overcome any selling phobias you may have and get out and do it. Selling doesn't have to mean getting people to buy junk that they don't need, but it may require educating the customer as to why they need something they never even heard of before. Don't confuse taking orders with selling. If somebody calls you on the phone and asks for a price or walks into your retail location and takes something off the shelf, you're no more of a sales-man than the counter help at a burger chain.

Many people hate dealing with salesmen of any kind, which is why personal relationships are so important. Once they've gotten past their pre-conceived loathing of you and begin to trust that you aren't out to rip them off for a quick buck, they'll want to deal with you to the exclusion of all other possible sources. That's why so many of the RFPs we mentioned earlier are written specifically for a sweet-heart vendor. It's not that dollars are changing hands under the table (though in some cases they may), it's that the customer doesn't want to deal with anybody else.

The first step in selling anything to anybody is to get their attention. This doesn't mean dressing up like a giant chicken and running around at the mall. It means getting in front of potential customers and quickly making a connection. If you've never done any selling before, you may want to write yourself a script and practice cold calling on the telephone to get used to rejection before you go out and get rejected in person. The first thing you'll learn is that you can't sell anything to the recep-tionist, except maybe a candy bar for a local little league team. Many people see receptionists as gatekeepers they'll never get past, but it's rarely the job of the receptionist to make business decisions. Simply ask for the purchasing or the IT (Information Technology) manager at bigger companies or "somebody in charge of buying computers" at smaller companies, and there's a good chance you'll get through to somebody you can practice your pitch on.

The next step is to ask questions. You're not going to get anywhere reeling off prices on the phone or talking about how great you are. You need a quick lead in like, "I'm Joe Shmo from

AAA Computers and I'm calling because . . . ." What comes after the "because" is the tricky part that you'll have to work out for yourself. It might be, "because we just opened an office around the corner from you" (yeah, around the corner and fifteen miles out of town on Route #66). It might be, "because we were just qualified as a higher education/state/you-name-it preferred vendor." It might be "because we've recently done a lot of business with companies in your field and we believe we can offer you very competitive services." Don't stop to catch your breath at this point, this was just the lead in. Now you have to establish some sort of relationship, and the best way to do this is to ask questions. "Could you tell me if you use local firms for computer service/training/hardware" (pick one specialty to pitch or you won't sound like a specialist!). "Have you purchased any PC equipment in the last six months?" "Does your current hardware/network vendor provide same day service?" You have to do at least a little homework about the people you're calling so you can guess which question to ask, because most people aren't going to stay on the phone for you to run through a whole laundry list. The final question, in any case, is "I'd love to come by and meet you in person. Is there a good time to catch you?" If you get to this stage and the person says "Yes," it doesn't guarantee you're going to sell anything, but it does mean you're on your way to becoming a salesperson.

Spending on Advertising

Advertising is not selling. Selling is active, advertising is passive. If you have money to spend on advertising, the most important thing you can do is spend it advertising to people who are likely to buy from you. Look, you could spend thousands of dollars on local TV spots targeting corporate customers, but they aren't going to do business with a nobody. They'll figure out how big you are in just two minutes of talking to you on the phone or by running a D&B (Dun and Bradstreet) on you if you're incorporated. You can go buy an expensive booth at an educator's convention and try to sell networked classrooms, but they have to go out to bid for anything they buy, so you're wasting your time. The first people to knock on your door trying to sell you advertising will be the local business magazine (every county has one), which survives on selling advertising to new businesses (and banks) and publishing feel good stories and interviews with local businessmen. Don't even consider it. It is a waste of money.

For a small business, the whole key to advertising is to focus on the product or service you most want to sell (i.e. the one you can really make money on), and to target the people who are most likely to buy it. You aren't a supermarket or a superstore chain, so you have no business trying to get people in the door with loss leaders. If you start selling your merchandise or services at what you hope is break-even just to get something going on, you'll usually lose your shirt. Likewise, the image advertising that is popular with large companies is a complete waste of money for the small guy. Unless you have a lot of money to spend on experiments, you should try to do a little market research on your target audience before you start. If you're interested in retail business, ask your friends and family what kinds of ads they pay attention to. If you're after business clients and you don't have any friends in businesses, take advantage of casual opportunities to ask questions as they present themselves, such as when you visit the doctor or make a purchase in a local business.

The best place for a new small business to put advertising dollars, particularly if you want to sell PC services and training to retail customers, is in copy shop flyers and tape. Often called Guerilla Marketing, this super inexpensive approach is ideally fitted to the small-scale computer business. Make up a flier on an 8.5"x11" paper that lists your services, prices, tells how friendly and responsive you are, and has ten or twelve separate tabs on the bottom with your name and phone number that can be torn off. The most common places to post these fliers are message boards in laundromats, university's hallways, and any other inside spaces with message boards, plus phone poles and traffic boxes in more liberal towns. Both the cost and effort to post the fliers is minimal, but again, make sure you know what you want to sell before you take the trouble to advertise it.

Direct mailing can be highly effective, providing you create a good mailing piece and you send it to the right people. One computer service entrepreneur I know reports great success building his business through mailings to local businesses. He started out by buying an inexpensive mailing list from the local Chamber of Commerce and picking out likely candidates, those businesses which would have several computers in their office but be too small to have a technician on staff. By designing the mailer as a postcard with a discount coupon on one side, he maximized the odds that it would catch the eye of the recipient and be saved, even if they didn't have any immediate service needs.

You should at least try to produce your own advertisements before getting involved with professionals. If nothing else, you'll have a better understanding of the factors involved when you go for help. One of the first consulting gigs I ever had was as a marketing advisor back in the late eighties for a successful clone company. They were doing several million a year in sales to end users and small businesses and wanted to take a shot at the corporate market. I prepared some product data sheets for them with the standard sales pitch on the front and technical specs on the back. I turned to a professional photographer whom a friend recommended to take the pictures, and one night the manager of this clone company and myself loaded up a van with hardware and drove to the photographer's home studio for pictures. Well, I popped my back adjusting the position of a giant 21" monitor and spent hours watching as the photographer clicked away, even posing the manager into some shots. I had neglected to formalize a plan for what we really wanted to shoot, and even worse, hadn't gotten a firm price for the job. In the end, we got a few useful prints, had to pay for several others at $35 apiece, and I ended up rebating part of my already low fee to make up for it. Always fix the scope of the job and the price before getting involved with outside professionals. Otherwise, you might get a $500 bill for what you thought was an interesting conversation with a lawyer or marketing consultant over coffee.

Inventory and Spoilage

Inventory is bad. Spoilage is even worse. Inventory is merchandise that you buy without having a customer, in order to have it in stock. Come the end of the year, inventory turns into a tax headache, and in the meantime, it's money that you've taken out of the bank and put on your shelves to devaluate. It's common knowledge that grocery stores and the restaurant industry suffer from spoilage, as the fresh foods they buy for inventory quickly go bad and must either be sold at a discount or tossed out. The computer industry also suffers from spoilage, both hardware and software,

Software spoilage occurs on a regular basis when new versions of the product appear. Software is usually returnable for credit if you buy it from a legitimate distributor and keep your eye on the ball. Don't get sucked into the notion that some customers are going to stick with a particular version of some software forever because it's reliable and does the job. Sooner or later, customers are forced to upgrade to current versions of software, and the old shrink wrapped boxes lose 100% of their value.

Hardware spoilage is more insidious, since the value creeps downwards day by day, rather than going into free fall. For example, when Intel releases a new CPU for the business/consumer market, the fastest model usually sells for around $500. A year later that same CPU will probably sell for around $100. The equivalent AMD CPU, which enters the market at around $250, will probably be obsolete by the end of the year, completely replaced by a new model. Obviously then, you don't want to buy quantities of high priced CPUs for stock, but how about something everybody always needs, like a hard drive? Well, the average hard drive has a shelf life of about a year, during which time it's price will fall by at least 50% and it will go from being the top capacity, top performer, to under performing. Unfortunately, as a small business, you can't afford to be stuck holding last year's hard drives, because the next step down the ladder is obsolescence. The same is true for almost all computer parts, including memory and motherboards, with the exceptions coming around the periphery. You probably won't suffer too much holding a modem or a video card in stock, and keyboards and mice have been holding their value since the price fell to under $20 for the pair. The point is, there's not a whole lot of difference between buying computer parts and lettuce. If you're making a big salad for a July 4th picnic, go nuts. Otherwise, don't buy more than you can eat in a couple days.

Shipping, Receiving, Returns

The main reason you need to worry about shipping in your small computer business is to return stuff. It might be to return unsold merchandise to a top tier distributor before the return period expires; it might be to return bad parts for warranty replacement; or it might be to return stuff that was shipped to you in error or doesn't meet your expectations. You may ship a self-sufficient customer the occasional replacement floppy drive or monitor, but chain stores like Staples have pretty much taken over the consumables business, meaning items like laser printer toner, inkjet cartridges and writeable CDs. There are really only two choices for shipping these days: UPS (United Parcel Service) and FedX (Federal Express). FedX now has a competitive ground delivery option, so you might want to pick whichever company has the closer office. Both UPS and FedX will bill you on a monthly basis and have all sorts of great package tracking services.

Receiving is what happens when UPS or FedX truck parks out front of your house or in back of your store and unloads a bunch of boxes on you. These services run a tight schedule, so don't expect to be able to open up the boxes and inspect the merchandise before you sign for them and watch the truck drive away. However, you can't leave stuff lying around unopened all day either, because that makes it much harder to push a "damaged in shipping" claim. All vendors will include a packing slip with the merchandise they ship you, which describes the items you have purchased, with or without pricing. An invoice will ship with the box if it's COD (Cash on Delivery). An invoice may also ship with the box if that merchandise is shipped on terms from an OEM, and sometimes that invoice is also your bill. Top tier distributors will normally invoice you separately by mail. Another difference between packing slips and invoices is that the serial numbers of the products you are buying often appear on the packing slip only. This packing slip serves as your receipt should you need to make a warranty return, while the invoice goes in the real receipts box for accounting and tax purposes. Depending on your relationship with the salesperson from whom you buy the merchandise, you may manage to have them dig up the paperwork (on their computer) necessary for you to make a warranty return, but you need to stay on their good side.

Returning merchandise for any reason requires that you first obtain a Return Merchandise Authorization (RMA). You must adapt yourself to the process of the vendor to obtain the RMA, usually through exchanging faxes or online. Once you have the RMA, you can ship the product out to the address they give you. If you have a good relationship with the vendor, you might ask for a cross-shipment, in which they send you a replacement part on your word that you are sending the defective part out to them simultaneously. Vendors are usually pretty generous in granting RMAs, but that doesn't mean that you should abuse the process by sending back parts at random when you're not really sure whether or not they're bad. If you do, you'll not only use up your goodwill in a hurry, you'll also run up a shipping bill. Distributors, who are middlemen by their nature, aren't particularly judgmental about the cause of component failure. Whether you send back a hard drive because it's failed in regular operation or because your new tech plugged the floppy drive power connector onto the master/slave select pins, they'll send it back to the manufacturer. I don't remember ever having been refused an RMA for a piece of brand name hardware, though I don't suppose I ever tried sending back stuff that had been dropped from a five story building.

R.M.A.- RETURN MERCHANDISE AUTHORIZATION

⛵ SELLING SERVICE

Earning a Good Reputation

Simple. Answer the phone, tell them when you'll have it ready or when you'll come over, and BE ON TIME. Trust me, in the end, being on time and making an effort means more to most customers than anything else. They understand that your time is your money, and that you don't want to be sitting at their computer re-installing Windows, so the fact that you came shows that you value them. I've hired and fired technicians over the years and the rarest quality to find is not technical competence, it's responsible behavior. Don't avoid your customers if things aren't going well, and don't give them optimistic projections of when you expect the parts to arrive or the job to be done. Always be realistic and straight with your customers, and if you're any good at your job, you'll succeed in making them happy. Making money, as we have noted, is another issue altogether, but it is a good time to point out that business customers aren't nearly as price sensitive as you might think. They don't want to be ripped off, but the important factor to them is that their computer procurement and operations shouldn't intrude on their ability to do business. They aren't in the computer business, they just want it to work. Dell has made a fortune selling the perception that they provide this kind of support, and they sell hardware at margins well exceeding the 20 points we talk about as a store-front minimum.

Just to draw the line a little clearer, let's take a moment to examine how you can earn a bad reputation and end up with legal problems. The number one way to really get your customers angry in any service business is to hide from them. This includes not answering the phone, not returning calls, not responding to e-mails, or making lame efforts to put in a showing at their establishment when you know they aren't going to be there.

If for some reason you get involved in a service problem you can't handle, tell the customer and help them find somebody else. Don't drag it out in the hopes that the situation will somehow resolve itself, because the eventual resolution can only be bad for you. In all the years I've worked in service, both hardware and software, the phrase I've used the most is "I don't know, but . . . ", which may be followed up with, " . . . but let's try this," or " . . . but I think I know where to find out," or " . . . but I'll take it back to the shop and work on it all night." The important thing is that the customer will appreciate your honesty and the special attention you are giving their problem, plus you'll have lowered their expectation for a miraculous solution. The truth is, by admitting you don't have the answer and then working the problem out quickly, you'll only enhance your reputation as a troubleshooter in the eyes of your customers. On the other hand, if you show up for a service call and find the whole problem is that the brightness on the monitor was turned down, or an icon was deleted from the desktop, don't try to make a big show of it to justify billing an hour. Whether you bill them or not depends on how tough you are (I'll admit to being a real softy on the one minute service call), but never fake that you're doing them some great service when you're not.

One of the worst practices you can get involved with in the service business is charging a new customer to go around their office poking into every machine and collecting data on the theory that this information is necessary to support them. When I worked as the technical editor for a PC hardware book in which an author kept pushing this practice, I wouldn't sign off on it. There is never any excuse to go around opening up healthy PCs and pulling out boards to write down the serial numbers and whatever settings you can identify. The only thing you can accomplish is to waste the customer's time and money, and very possibly to mess up a computer in the process. There's no advantage in knowing what's inside a working PC that you didn't sell the customer. If it fails, you'll have plenty of time to see what's inside when you go out to identify the problem. Unfortunately, the practice of creating these control sheets for PCs is ingrained with some old school techs who don't even realize that they are perpetrating a rip-off. Just don't do it.

Field Service

Buy a good screwdriver, the kind with the hollow shaft that has a dual ended Philips bit on one end and a dual ended standard bit on the other. Carry it in your pocket with the wide Philips bit projecting (all the others are likely to puncture clothing and skin if you sit down wrong), or take the bit out and carry it loose in the pocket. It beats the hell out of the screwdrivers with the ten bits in the circular rubber holder that like to fall out into the computers you're working on, and with the exception of network crimping tools, it's the only tool you should ever need.

Don't try and stock or carry inventory to fix any problem that comes up on the theory that you'll save time. The most you should carry in the trunk is a 1.44 MB floppy drive and cable, a cheap IDE CD ROM and cable, AGP and PCI video adapters, a keyboard, mouse, a generic modem and some RAM – the most generic SIMM and DIMM you have. Hard drive failures are so catastrophic to the average user that replacing it on the spot is rarely the issue. Monitors and bigger peripherals can usually be "borrowed" from another machine on site, if you're pleasant about it. If the repair is a warranty repair on equipment you sold, you'll have to use your judgement as to equivalent parts, because the RMA process is too slow to make your customer wait. If the service call is for hardware you didn't sell, always leave the customer the defective part you replace. Don't hesitate to bring the PC back to your shop, unless you are positive you have the problem figured out. Running back and forth kills time and nerves. Be careful of static, but remember that most new PCs are never entirely off unless unplugged, so it's better to unplug them and not shuffle your feet around, than to work with them plugged in and wonder why the motherboard died.

Most field service problems, if they don't turn out to be a stone-dead piece of hardware, involve a software component. Troubleshooting software issues is a tough nut for everybody, but particularly difficult for new technicians with limited experience. Your best friend, when it comes to dealing with specific error messages is Google. When confronted with an error message for which you don't have an immediate fix, don't waste time on hold trying to call the software company – that's your last option. Hop on the web, go to Google, and put the error message in quotes, like: "System policies do not allow adding the selected device." My brother-in-law's computer expert

EFFICIENT SPEAKER PHONE USE

called me with that error one night after he spent a couple hours trying to troubleshoot why a computer on the office network could see the server but not communicate. I hung up (no broadband access), popped the error into Google, and got exactly four hits. Three were error reports with no solution, but one was an answer (a bit set wrong in the registry), with precise instructions for fixing it. My brother-in-law believes I'm a genius, but now you know better! I've even used Google to track down the physical location of a fuel pump relay on a 1987 Mustang LX. It was easy enough to pinpoint the problem with the Chilton schematics, but try actually finding the relay on the car (turned out to be under the drivers seat, mounted against the floor pan towards the back seat!).

What this means for the modern technician, is that after your screwdriver, the most important tool you can carry is a notebook computer. Some clients will only have one computer at their location and, since you're there, it probably isn't working. Even if they have multiple computers in an office, it's not very professional to start kicking their employees off their machines so you can surf the web for answers. It doesn't have to be a good notebook, though it should have enough life left in the battery to handle a half-hour online without needing the AC adapter. Finding a power outlet to plug into near the phone jack can be a bigger challenge than finding the problem solution once you get on the web. It's also critical that you have a reliable Internet Service Provider to call, because you don't want to be fighting with busy signal when you dial-up. The notebook also needs to have a working floppy drive, in case the solution involves downloading an updated driver or a patch from the web. This means you have to keep the virus checking software on the notebook up-to-date, since the last thing you need is to introduce a virus into your client's office.

Supporting networks, office software, and other specialty software products in the field is usually a blend of service and training. The longer you've worked for a particular customer, the quicker you'll be able to resolve their problems. For one thing, you'll get to know the weaknesses of their systems, but more importantly, you'll have educated the customer in how to describe their problems, which is the most critical component of successful service. Network configuration requires more experience than most other types of software setup, and you should really run a copy of whatever network software you are supporting in your home/office, even if it's only one PC and a server. For my money, the most important thing you can do for a customer whose network you are supporting is to make sure that their backups are working. In these days of Internet connectivity and viruses, you also need to keep an eye out for special patches for security flaws that appear with such regularity. The most common tasks in network configuration and maintenance after the initial install are adding new users, new software, and software upgrades. The upgrades could be patches to the network operating system, or new versions of applications software.

Many people would consider telephone support as separate from field service, but as far as I'm concerned, it's field service using remote eyes and hands to do the work. Whether or not you charge for the time depends on whether it's warranty or service contract work, your relationship with the customer, and how long you spend on the phone. For detailed software support, it always pays to be sitting in front of a computer screen yourself and going through the steps you are describing over the phone, rather than having to ask the customer to describe every screen they are looking at in minute detail. When it comes to hardware troubleshooting over the phone, if you can keep them on the line until you've fixed the problem or precisely determined the source, you're on your way to a successful career. Always start with the obvious when troubleshooting over the phone, because the odds that you and your customer are on the same wavelength are pretty low. A simple example would be a customer calling up and saying that they can't access the Internet. If the only thing that customer uses the computer for is to access the Internet, it might be that when he turned on the power switch, nothing happened, and to him that means that he can't access the Internet. The first step in any remote troubleshooting is to get the person on the other end of the line to establish for you what DOES work, and from there, you can move on to what doesn't.

I'm differentiating between service and product development here, which we'll get to in the next chapter. Field service is generally limited to when something that used to work a certain way stops working. For example, the network printer no longer prints from a particular work station, a Word file has mysteriously reverted to an earlier version, nobody can access the G: drive on the server, or the e-mail isn't getting through. Sometimes these problems will creep up without any human involvement, say a hard drive running out of room, or a pre-set limit on the number of files being reached. More often these problems will have their source in some human error, such as the accidental deletion of a file or an attempt to restore a single file from a tape backup actually restoring the entire volume.

Service Contracts

The steadiest income stream you can derive comes from service contracts. I'll admit up front that I have never sold any service contracts while in business for myself, for the simple reason that I travel overseas for several months every year, which puts an obvious limit on my availability. There are several basic ways to structure a service contract, from a relatively low monthly fee to be available for some minimum amount of phone support, to a substantial monthly payment to take full responsibility for keeping a computer installation in a business up and running, including parts cost. The downside of service contracts, of course, is that you'll have to be available to at least call the customer back in a reasonable amount of time after being beeped or receiving a phone message. Years ago, it was common to promise a 4 hour response time (that you'd actually be on the customer site within 4 hours), but as you can imagine, that puts an incredible number of restrictions on the owner/operator of a one person business. While it's possible to find other local computer professionals to back you up, a role I've frequently filled for others, it's probably better not to guarantee to be on site during the same business day unless your sole focus will be on the service business. Many customers are open to having you come in after office hours and on weekends to do service work, and weekends are really the only time you want to get involved in serious upgrades to software or hardware. If you want to learn all about service contracts, including how to price them, buy the book *From Serf to Surfer: Becoming a Network Consultant* by Strebe et al, ISBN: 0782126618

Shop Service

I'm not a lawyer, but I always worry more about liability when people leave stuff overnight than when I go to their place to work on it. You may want to buy a "Merchandise Ticket" pad with a disclaimer of responsibility for customers to sign when you accept hardware for service, but in the end, I figure if lawyers get involved, you lose even if you win. I've never been sued; politeness and honesty probably help.

Most service issues are pretty obvious, and this isn't a dissertation on building or repairing PCs. The main risk in shop service is taking on repair of intermittent freeze-ups on hardware you didn't sell. Why is this such a risk? The problem, unless it's a computer virus, will be hardware based. After observing the freeze-up in your shop, you'll make your best guess, or put your faith in some diagnostics software, and replace something: motherboard, CPU, RAM, hard-drive, power supply, video, you name it. You keep the machine around for a day, and if it doesn't freeze again, you return it to the customer with a bill for the part and your time. Two days later you get a call that the problem has recurred. You get it back and repeat the process, same result. Do you refund for parts and swap old parts back in? Do you rebate some time? Do you give up? It really depends on your schedule and how important that customer is to you. Intermittent failures of some types are nightmares, and the best solution is to avoid taking them on at all.

Shop rates are lower than field rates; $50/hr is a reasonable shop rate for most regions, with a minimum one-hour charge. Most repairs won't take anywhere near an hour, but dealing with the customer and the paperwork often will. A man I once worked with had been the head of service for a national computer retailer, and he used to lead technicians through the following ritual Q&A. "What does a technician fix?" he would ask. "The customer," was the answer he wanted. This notion of "fixing the customer," i.e., doing whatever it takes to make them leave you alone, includes fixing the blame on Microsoft or some other software vendor, or even worse, convincing the customer that they lack some mystical "computer ability" and it's their fault. "Fixing the customer" is a terrible way to run a service department. Fix the problems, not the customers, and the customers will fix themselves.

Selling Upgrades

If you ask me, upgrading PCs is a nasty business for both the tech and the customer. The days of simple upgrades, like adding a modem or a CD-ROM, are long gone, since just about every PC sold in the last five years will have full multimedia capabilities. What most customers are looking for is more memory, more hard drive space, and a faster CPU. The simplest of these to perform is the memory upgrade, particularly on brand-name machines. Armed with the make and model of a brand-name PC, you can go to a website like kingston.com or crucial.com and get a guaranteed compatible component. Most clones use generic SIMMs or DIMMS, and these have gotten so cheap that the best way to do an upgrade is to buy the amount of memory the customer wants installed and completely replace the currently installed RAM. While I've occasionally had trouble finding RAM that will properly register on some odd-ball motherboards, it's certainly the easiest upgrade of the big three.

The problem with upgrading hard drives is not the mechanical fit but transferring the software. Most customers won't call for a hard drive upgrade until the original drive is so filled up that it's causing crashes. This means that simply adding the new hard drive as a second drive won't fix the problem, and besides, the customer wouldn't see any performance gain on boot up if you leave the old boot drive as C:. However, simply copying the contents of the old drive to the new and then setting the new drive bootable usually doesn't work out easily unless you use a third-party software package to do the job. In any case, the whole process always takes longer than you expect, and that's time you have to bill the customer.

The most problematic upgrade is the CPU/motherboard, since you'll rarely encounter an old motherboard capable of running a new enough CPU to make the upgrade worthwhile. The immediate difficulty with replacing the motherboard is that the video adapter may require upgrading also, and some older slot types for other adapters may no longer be supported. You'll have to reinstall all the Windows drivers, assuming Windows will even boot and let you access the CD without excessive work. Again, it's no big deal if you're doing it as a hobby, but can you justify charging a customer several hours, and maybe ending up with something that permanently remains a little temperamental at boot time?

All that aside, when most people ask for a PC upgrade, what they're really shooting for is to get a new PC on the cheap. Unfortunately, this usually means you'll have to replace everything except for the case, power supply, floppy drive, keyboard and mouse. Taken together they are worth maybe $50, or one hour of your inexpensive field service rate, which won't be enough time to do the job. This all assumes that you can sell the individual upgrade components to the customer at the same price as you could if you were selling them built into a PC, which you can't. Why? Upgraded machines generate more service calls then new machines, and the customer will be convinced that any problem that arises is a direct result of your still-under-warrantee upgrade and not a coincidental failure. When all is said as done, you're better off educating your customers in the cost effectiveness of buying new PCs and donating the old ones to charity, if they can find a charity that wants them.

Selling Training

I'm don't enjoy stand-up teaching, so I've never gone after training as a market. I have done a lot of one-on-one training and even thought of billing myself as a PC therapist at one point, since helping older people get over their fear of computers turned into something of a specialty, albeit a revenue free one. Most business training is done in a classroom environment, with anywhere from four to twenty students sitting in front of PCs and following along with the trainer. Classroom training requires a set curriculum, workbooks and study materials, and plenty of preparation. The one thing classroom training does not necessarily require, oddly enough, is certification in the subject that the trainer is teaching. It's another example of how showing up and doing the job is more important than any certificate. Freelance trainers can earn hundreds of dollars an hour, or thousands of dollars per day, but it does require presentation skills that many computer geeks lack.

One-on-one training is a much easier market to break into, and can either be billed at your regular field service rate or separately negotiated. You don't need a fixed curriculum or training materials to teach one-on-one, though they can help you structure the time and feel confident about what you are doing. I recently met a guy overseas who had built up a healthy one-on-one training business, despite the fact he wasn't fluent in the local lingo. His favorite tool (and emotional support) was a short training manual for Windows and basic Office functions he had put together; a 20 page copy shop job, which he sold his clients for cost. It had the effect of raising his stature in their eyes (hey, this guy has his stuff together), plus it allowed him to keep his trainees focused on the things he felt were important to get up and running. If you don't supply any training materials, your students will probably go out and buy one of those poorly written 300 page or longer "Blank made easy" type books, which try to cover every option on every pull-down menu. Then, when you show up to try to teach them something useful, they will be hopelessly bogged down in details they'll never need, and you will have lost the chance to keep them on target.

The most important thing you can do when training an individual is to always have them drive (i.e., never take over the mouse or the keyboard to get something done quickly), and to give as few directions as possible. Most people learn through doing, not through listening, and if you give them such detailed instructions that they don't even have to think, they won't get much done when you aren't sitting next to them. For example, if somebody has never used Windows before, the first couple times you tell them to click on "File," you might need to add "top left of the screen." After the second or third time, if they aren't quickly finding it themselves, just wait until they do. Another good rule is to explain early on that many tasks will require them to click on "OK" or "CONTINUE" and not continually prompt them to do this. If you ever encounter adults who have never used a computer in their lives, you'll find that one of their weakest points is what basketball coaches call "court vision," seeing the whole court. These clients often fail to see pop-up windows that appear on the screen even if they are looking right at them, and will try to print a document a dozen times without ever acknowledging the pop-up window that asks how many copies you want to print.

The worst thing you can do as a trainer is to fail to gauge the reaction of the students to your teaching and make the necessary adjustments. I've participated in training sessions where the lead trainer was exclusively focused on covering the material he'd prepared, and would argue with the students about what they needed to know. If somebody is paying you to learn how to use a word processor, you can't spend a half and hour on how files are stored on the hard drive before you get to basic formatting. My approach, when teaching any computer application to somebody who lacks any experience in saving and organizing files, is to wait for them to ask me questions. No modern software application will let you exit without prompting "Do you want to save?," so you can be sure the question will come up. Rather than getting into directory structure in the first session, just let the files fall where the application naturally puts them, and reserve organizational issues for when the student has mastered the basic application functions, which is what they're paying you for.

Certification

Amazon sells over 1,000 different books on how to pass certification tests for computer products, primarily software. While the average customer walking into your PC shop isn't going to ask you whether you've earned this or that certification, many companies do use certification as a filter, particularly when hiring consultants. I've never heard of anybody getting a job simply because they had passed a certification test, but if two otherwise equivalent consultants are angling for the same work and only one is certified in the product the job revolves around, it will probably make the difference. Training people to pass certification tests is a big business, for both trainers and publishers. Perhaps the most important role of certification to the consultant is as a confidence builder, so you don't feel like you're walking into your sales pitch naked.

Another place certification plays a role is in signing up to do warranty service for brand-name manufacturers. Some of these won't even consider your application unless you have two or three A+ certified technicians on staff. Oddly enough, these same manufacturers may outsource some of their warranty work to national warranty brokers. These brokers function by contacting local PC shops all over the country and soliciting their help with warranty service, usually with no certification requirements. Just keep in mind that certifications are obtained through taking multiple choice tests. Even though these tests are appreciably more difficult to pass than the learner's permit exam for a driver's license, they include no "hands-on" component. If you try to hire technicians based entirely on the number of certifications they have, you could easily end up with somebody who can't parallel park.

Public Relations

Public relations is the art of advertising without paying for it. The main point of PR is to get your name out in front of people in any context related to your business. If you hire a PR agency, and there are affordable mom 'n mom PR agencies in every city, you end up paying for the service, but not for the actual exposure. The secret to PR is in understanding that media outlets, especially print, need content, something to fill their pages with. Everybody understands that the "human interest" stories on the local TV station are great free advertising for somebody when they touch on a business, but few people realize how much of the local print news is actually transcribed from press releases. In order to pass your advertising off as a news item, you have to make it "newsworthy" and write the press release such that a paper can use it with little or no modification. A basic news story must contain the five "wh's": who, what, when, where and why. It should never include pricing information, which makes it look too much like an ad unless it's going in the business section, and it should be tied into the immediate present. In other words, a story about how your company won preferred city vendor status six months ago is no good, but a story describing your first six months of sales on the city contract might make it into the local business section.

Study your local papers, particularly the weekly tabloids that are often inserted in the Sunday paper or handed out free in supermarkets, and never be afraid to call an editor on the phone. Some papers specialize in "feel good" stories, so they're more interested in your volunteer work, teaching or donating computer service at the old folks home or orphanage, than how much square footage you just rented in the local business incubator. On the other hand, the technology or science page editor will be more interested in your being the first kid on the block with the new Intel processor or a solar powered battery charger for notebooks. Even without staging special events or taking on volunteer work, you'll see that the potential for regular free publicity is almost limitless if you are clever about it. However, if you can't write, it's a lost cause to try it yourself, so you'll have to consider hiring a pro. Stick with somebody who works out of their home and is willing to be paid based solely on results, like so much per news item that appears. The rule of thumb for small business is that you can't afford a PR firm with a receptionist or with leather chairs in the office. Also, be realistic in the publications you target. You aren't going to get a press release into the New York Times or the Wall Street Journal, and even if you did by some miracle, you wouldn't be reaching your potential customers, who are local.

Confederation

Anybody who has ever seen a cop show on TV understands the danger of going into an unknown situation without backup. So where does a sole proprietor without employees turn for backup? In my experience, the best answer is unofficial confederation with other independents whose skills don't overlap your own any more than necessary. First of all, unless you have limited faith in your ability to handle problems in the area you are specializing in, you don't need somebody with the identical skill set behind you. Secondly, if you have to start calling for help when doing what you're supposed to be best at, your customers might figure out they don't need you as a middleman and hire your backup. The point of confederation is to expand your ability to do business by having available expertise in areas you aren't strong in or would prefer not to work in. Any time you form an official relationship, it's an occasion to try a press release on the local paper, detailing your backgrounds and your new enterprise.

Some professionals, such as trainers or networking experts, may prefer to pay you a finders fee for bringing them into a job, but retain their own identity and billing. Others might be willing to function as subcontractors, or hired guns, billing you their professional courtesy rate, and leaving you to bill the customer. If two (or more) of you are pitching a new customer together or responding to a bid that neither could take on alone, a more formal written arrangement will probably be required. In any case, it's a good idea to do a little business with local people in your field, just to get to know them. That way if some emergency arises, like your spouse forcing you to take a vacation after three years of seven-day weeks, you'll already have somebody you're comfortable with lined up to handle your service issues.

⚓ PRODUCT DEVELOPMENT

Value Added Reseller and Strategic Partnerships

The most basic level of computer product development is buying a software package, buying a PC, installing the software on the PC, and selling it as a product. Stupid as that may sound, it covers a lot of the Value Added Reseller (VAR) and Strategic Partnership markets, and it's not a bad business to be in. By filling out a bunch of paperwork for the actual software manufacturer and possibly attending a seminar or some classes, they'll provide you with sales leads in your area and steep discounting off the retail price of software. Your value as a "partner" is providing the outside sales, delivery and installation, and the first level of technical support. The obvious drawback is that you'll have plenty of competition in popular software packages, much of it from established companies.

The next higher level on the VAR food chain is providing serious customization and scripting, something well beyond setting up word processor templates that include the company letterhead. Actually, on the subject of word processors and office suites, don't turn your nose up at setting up mail merges and simple databases. Even if these customizations seem minor to you, your customers probably don't want to be in the computer software business, and might not even know such options exist. More serious scripting can result in great time savings for your clients, eliminating large numbers of keystrokes on routine tasks, the sort of job that was once accomplished through batch files. Because customization work is regarded as a specialty, it is usually billed at a higher rate, typically $75 and hour or more. Established companies won't do anything on site for less than $100/hr, so here you have a pricing advantage. As with any type of consulting service, the more hours the job will take, the lower the rate you can charge

The top of the VAR chain is actually developing software add-ons that appreciably enhance the basic product, or to adapt it to a completely different purpose. A good example of this is a friend of mine who started a company to provide speech recognition software to doctors and lawyers, who pay tens of thousands of dollars a year for transcription services. The basic products he sells, Dragon Simply Speaking and IBM Via Voice, are pretty good at basic speech-to-text right out of the shrink-wrapped box. In order to enhance the usefulness of the product to doctors, my friend has developed custom vocabularies of thousands of medical terms unique to several specialties in the medical field. This appreciably shortens the time a doctor will need to spend training the software and improves the accuracy, both of which increase the chances of a happy customer. Other customizations include scripts to perform billing, mail merges, and database entries.

Franchises

If you are looking to jumpstart your business identity and product line, one option is to obtain a franchise. I have no direct experience with computer franchises, but the approach seems to be picking up steam. A little research on the Internet turned up a half-dozen franchise operations with professional websites, complete with maps showing current franchise locations. Prices for franchises ranged from $8,000 to $45,000, with the majority falling near the more expensive end of the scale. Monthly fees of a few hundred dollars were also part of some deals. Franchise models ranged from retail locations in shopping malls to a cell-phone dispatched repair business that could be run out of the trunk of a car. All of the franchisers offer a whole laundry list of benefits, most of which are of small or questionable value.

I can't think of a more expensive and risk laden path into the computer business than buying a franchise, so you had better come up with a list of questions to ask. Insist on satisfactory answers up front – don't settle for "that's competitive information that we can't possibly give you until you sign up." I would start with asking how many franchisees they currently have, what the average first full year income was for those franchisees, and what percentage of people who purchased franchises are still doing it for their primary business. Get these numbers in writing. Ask for the names of the franchisees nearest you and visit them. I wouldn't put much faith in what a regional "Master" franchisee has to say, since these people have a vested interest in signing you up. You want to talk to franchisees who are operating at the level you will be on. If visiting existing franchisees involves using up a week of vacation from your day job, or appreciable travel expenses, I'd still do it. To buy a franchise, we're talking about amounts of money that would pay for a condo in some places – would you buy a condo sight unseen? Find out how long the franchiser has been in business, and if they are a public company, check out their financial statements in Dun&Bradstreet at the nearest library that subscribes to the Million Dollar Database.

An important exercise is to go down the list of "advantages" they are offering you and put a value on each. One of the first things most franchisers will offer you is an exclusive territory. Well, last time I checked 100% of nothing is still nothing. There have to be a dozen McDonalds within driving distance of most places I've lived, so if somebody offered me a franchise that covered my whole state, I'd assume that something fishy is going on. Another big selling point for franchisers is business documentation. I could take this book, transfer it onto 8.5 x 11 sheets in a loose leaf binder and include bulleted items at the beginning of each chapter. Would that make it worth thousands of dollars? Business materials are another selling point: stationery, printed t-shirts, a starter kit of spare parts, possibly a couple hundred dollars worth of stuff you could easily have found locally (and met local business owners in the bargain). Franchise deals normally include a couple days of initial training (you pay for travel and lodging). Find out exactly what the training will consist of, including an hourly class schedule, and determine how much of it is actually relevant for you. In other words, if you're already a great tech or trainer, you aren't going to derive any benefit from a beginner's course on this subject. Count the hours for whatever remains, and assign a reasonable value, certainly less than a hundred dollars an hour. Check with your local unemployment office or community college to find out about the availability of equivalent or more comprehensive training in your area, to give you a point of comparison. Another questionable value is help with start-up advertising, press releases, etc.. They're talking about giving you some canned press releases and ads, not tailoring a campaign for you, and if they actually pay for any advertising, rest assured that they're doing it with a portion of the money you've forked over.

Leads and referrals are the plum of any VAR type relationship, but can a franchiser generate real leads for you? This is why it's so crucial to actually visit and talk with some current franchisees, to find out how much business they are getting as a direct result of their having laid out a ton of money. I'm not aware of any computer franchisers who have a national reputation or media presence, something that would lead a customer to pick your number from the yellow pages over somebody else's. If the deal involves a retail location and branded merchandise that can be sold for a substantial markup, you should take this into account. There's no question that franchising as a business model can be hugely successful for all parties, I just haven't seen it work in the computer industry.

My negative tilt on the whole subject of laying out money for a business relationship should be obvious, and while I've never been directly involved in a computer franchise, I have seen a lot of "nothing for something" transactions. There are all sorts of products and business models that have failed in the retail world, only to be recycled as "opportunities" for new businesses to break in with. I'm always suspicious when I see some guy on TV who claims to know how to make millions in real estate trying to sell me cassette tapes on how I can do the same for just $49.95 – in three easy credit card payments. Somebody in your family or community might help you get a start in business from the goodness of their heart, but when it comes to paying tens of thousands of dollars to some corporate entity, you better make real sure you're going to get your money's worth.

Informational Websites

The primary difference between informational and commercial websites is that informational websites are much easier to set up and don't need to be integrated into the customer's existing IT infrastructure. An informational website can either be a magnet to draw new customers (i.e. advertising), or the equivalent of a business card on the web, a placeholder where somebody looking for your customer will be able to find their contact information, including a phone number and e-mail address. A good informational website must be designed to attract the maximum amount of useful traffic, and part of this process requires regular tweaking of the site content, in response to the traffic flow. This absolutely requires that the site be hosted on a commercial server that provides useful usage statistics on a daily basis. You can get a commercial host for as little as $1/month, though you won't get any phone support at that level. I prefer finding a host with a human being who answers the phone, and this will usually run around $10 a month.

When you set out to design an informational website, one or more sit-down meetings with the client is a necessity. I usually start by showing the customer usage statistics from one of my own websites, to drive home the point that the vast majority of traffic is driven by search engines. Then I take them to Google or AltaVista and ask them what sort of queries they would put into a search engine if they were looking for their products or services. By studying the construction of the pages that come up, both the on-screen text and the hidden Metatags, you should be able to construct a site that will also show up in the top ten returns, with two caveats. First, Google, which is currently the 800 lb. guerilla of the search engines, gives some weight to how many other quality sites link to a given site, on the theory that a heavily linked site must have useful content. Second, many other search engines have ceased to be fair markets, and simply sell top positions to the highest bidder. There's nothing you can do about the second problem, but one way to rapidly overcome the first is to exchange links with related sites, but not so closely related that you'll be sending your clients business to them. The best sites to get your customer listed in are quality directory sites, since they don't ask for reciprocal links and don't have any content that will compete with your client's.

The price you can charge for simple website design has been dropping ever since the Internet bubble burst a couple years ago. If you enjoy doing web work, you might even do it for a lower price than your shop rate for fixing PCs. If the site is going to take you more than an hour or two, try to involve the customer as much as possible in the artistic design, and establish regular progress milestones for the customer to sign off on. That might not sound like very much fun, but it beats putting in twenty hours before the customer gets their first look and says, "Oooh, I don't like that very much at all." Another drawback is that the customer may confuse you with the ISP, even if you have them contract the hosting service on their own, and insist on calling you for support on issues that you have no control over. There's nothing wrong with functioning as a middleman between the customer and the ISP as long as the time is billable.

Commerce Websites

Commerce Websites are sites which allow you to order products online, using a credit card on retail sites and an account and password on business-to-business (B2B) sites. I've never set up a B2B site, and I'm not going to try to snow you into thinking I have, but I'll throw out a couple general comments on the subject. B2B customers aren't simply looking for an online catalog, they're trying to achieve cost savings through streamlining operations and cutting out both paperwork and people. These systems must be fully integrated into whatever enterprise software the company is running to be effective. For example, a proper B2B implementation will remove stock from inventory as it is sold, and even initiate orders for replacement stock when it's needed.

Commerce websites take much longer to design and have much more stringent performance requirements than informational websites, so I wouldn't undertake to do one without a written contract. Your first contract should always be written with the help of a lawyer; afterwards it may be possible to recycle the boilerplate for new customers with very minor modifications. When performance milestones are reached and demonstrated to the customer, they should also be billed – don't settle for "payment on conclusion of the work." Rates for designing commerce websites vary greatly with how many unemployed programmers there are in your area, but you can take the average rate for contract programmers from the Sunday Help Wanted and use that for a base.

Retail commerce sites are much simpler to set up, and most web hosts offer some sort of all-in-one package deal with a merchant bank to process credit card orders on a secure server. Orders entered into an online form are forwarded to the site owner by simple e-mail, and order fulfillment is carried out the same as if the order was placed over the phone. On one particularly badly designed website, I ordered an item, entering all of my credit card information, phone number, shipping address, etc, but noticed that the shipping charge wasn't displayed online. The next day I got a long distance call from them. It turned out that this outfit called everybody on the phone to ask what type of shipping they wanted, which sort of blows the whole point of having a commerce website!

Be a Little Paranoid

E-mail is 100% reliable, right? WRONG! If you send an e-mail to somebody and their service is messed up, at least you'll get failed delivery notice, right? WRONG! If a website goes down for any reason, the hosting service will contact all of the site owners and tell them, right? WRONG! After you've built a lovely site for your client and submitted the address to a couple of search engines, the job is over, right? WRONG, WRONG, WRONG. Websites require regular care and feeding, not to mention continual monitoring, so when you sell website development, you should try to sell a service contract to pay for a couple hours a month of your time. These hours can be spent tweaking the design, watching the usage stats, resubmitting to search engines, and most importantly, making sure the site is up and the e-mail is working.

My writing site, fonerbooks, was hosted for its first year on a cheap web service that I knew only from their commerce website. When I was traveling, I wanted to have e-mail roving capabilities on the site, so I enabled the switch that was supposed to support that feature and forgot about it. For the next two weeks, all of my incoming mail disappeared into a black hole, never to be recovered. I was so ticked off, not only by this but by the complete absence of technical support, that I decided to move the site to my local commercial web host, with whom I'd hosted my business site for over five years. After endless headaches wresting the URL away from my unresponsive original host, everything appeared set. I tested out my e-mail addresses, then sent out review copies of the translations I'd just published with my e-mail as the sole contact information. You see, despite my recent problems, I still thought e-mail was pretty bulletproof.

Well, within a couple days of my sending out these review copies, a one shot affair like a debutante's ball, my reliable Internet Service Provider (ISP), upgraded their e-mail software. Over the next couple weeks, I still received e-mail addressed to my account at the ISP, but the catch-all for mail sent to the domain, like morris@fonerbooks.com, had failed. I wondered at not receiving any e-mail from people who had asked for review copies of the book, but it wasn't until somebody went to the trouble of tracking down my phone number and calling me that I found out what was happening. Again, for a multi week period, any email sent to my domain had disappeared into a black hole, never to be recovered. My ISP was incredulous, but I sent myself several test messages from other accounts and never received bounce messages for failed delivery. Whoever sent me e-mail in that period probably thinks I'm a jerk to this day. The problem, by the way, turned out to be that an employee at the ISP had forgotten the carriage return after my domain name, which was at the end of a file the new e-mail software was using.

Consulting and Contract Programming

The only difference between a software consultant and a contract programmer is that programmers actually work for a living. Just kidding, but consultants are generally involved in helping management with "big picture" issues, such as what software to buy, how to implement new enterprise systems with a minimum of disruption, and how to best coordinate and manage other outside contractors, such as programmers. Consulting is nowhere near as glamorous as it sounds, because most consultants actually work for Fortune 500 companies, live in motels, and get yelled at a lot for doing such a poor job. Consultants deserve most of the abuse they take from customers, since they charge a lot of money and over-promise, which frequently results in companies abandoning projects after investing millions of dollars in development.

Contract programming is a far more honorable profession, not surprising I should say so since I've done a reasonable amount of it. Such jobs frequently require a full time presence at the customer site, at least in the initial stages, so it doesn't always fit well with the more standard computer business model. The best source for programming work that you can take on without abandoning the rest of your business is from your regular customers. While helping a friend close out some hardware business after his company failed, I literally fell into the longest running programming gig I ever had. The client was a large wastewater treatment plant that had invested serious bucks in some process control software, Intellutions, but didn't have anybody on staff with the background to implement it. The job stretched over five years, as more areas of the plant were added to the system. The highest rate I ever charged them was $35/hour, since I was learning on the job and they were 100% flexible as to when and how I did the work. When I decided the time had come to move on and started looking for another professional who would be willing to come in and handle small upgrades to the system, I couldn't find any takers at $100/hour. The moral of the story is, if you price your time reasonably in order to learn an industry standard software package with industrial applications, you can earn a steady income and increase your worth at the same time.

Original Software Products

At the risk of repeating myself yet again, the hard part of the software business isn't the software, it's the business. Back in the early 90's when CD ROMs were a relatively new phenomena, I invested a couple thousand dollars in a CD Recorder and some image capture hardware and took a stab at the educational software business. I made one fatal mistake and I made it right at the beginning. I decided I would handle the technical side and would find a partner with "content" which could be adapted for a CD ROM. In order to prove my worth to potential partners, I spent a month or so creating a prototype nature CD, creatively titled "Trees." The CD contained images of trees native to the Connecticut River Valley, along with some descriptive text, audio (including snatches of tree related poetry I read from books, such as "No wars did men molest, when only beech'n bowls were in request.") and a tree identification game. I did all of the programming in Visual Basic Professional, which had just added some Windows supported multimedia features. The images of trees I shot with a borrowed camcorder at Smith College, since they had the good sense to attach metal identification tags including the Latin names to all the interesting trees on the campus. So, not realizing that I had really created a product by myself, I started looking around for "content" partners.

My first partnership, nothing written on paper, was with an author who had published a popular book on the natural history of the region and had excellent success selling in the public schools that were my target market. I put in about six weeks of seven days a week doing a prototype CD, including fake bird calls and animated sequences of pictures, so we could do a little market research and maybe raise some money for a highly polished version. What ensued was almost comic. My partner was so impressed with the prototype that he wanted to forget about doing a CD for the local area and jump right into the natural history of New York or Boston. He was concerned that somebody would steal our ideas and we would lose out on the more lucrative markets. I pointed out that neither of us had been in the educational CD business before and that it would be a good idea to work the bugs out on a small scale before betting the ranch. The next week he was back with the idea that we should drop the whole natural history thing and do a product based on all the free photographs NASA would supply to anybody who asked. Not surprisingly, there were already a number of NASA CDs on the market, at least one of which was put together by a team of Russian astrophysicists. At this point, I told him it wasn't working out and wrote-off the time I'd invested.

Failing to learn from my mistake, I went hunting for another "content" partner and found a university professor with an impressive slide collection of trees. For a second time, I went with a paperless partnership, offering to bring the product along to a point where we could evaluate the commercial potential. Well, I guess I was just a stupid thirty-year old who hadn't gotten enough abuse in graduate school. I spent about three months building a database from his slide collection along the same lines of my original "Trees" prototype, with most of the time going into photo editing and cropping. What I failed to realize was that it wasn't a business for my partner, and he didn't understand that there was a difference between what I was doing and what his funded students were working on. Nor had I realized that there were holes in his collection, which would take a minimum of a year to fill in while waiting for the seasonal changes, providing that he went out there and did it. When I dropped the project, I doubt he understood what a disaster it had been to me in financial terms, since I had to give up on software development and get some paying work.

One good thing did come out of my experiences in trying to become a multimedia tycoon. I discovered if you're capable of doing 90% of a job, you're better off learning how to do the other 10% than taking on a partner of any kind. When I sold my first computer book to McGraw-Hill, it never even occurred to me to find a professional photographer as a co-author. Instead, I borrowed a decent 35mm camera from a friend and taught myself how to take photographs. I've since had well over 500 photographs published in four books. On the downside, that expensive CD Recorder I bought died of old age a few years later, and I doubt I recorded enough CD's to get the cost under $100 apiece!

Building PCs from Scratch

If you are going into the computer business because you just can't get enough of building PCs, you'll probably want to do it from scratch. This works out best in a retail location, since you need to fill the space with something anyway, you can let the customers choose from a whole variety of attractively displayed cases and motherboards. Keep the motherboards under glass. Static risk aside, excessive handling can't do them any good. You can keep other parts out in retail boxes, but I wouldn't encourage customer handling of anything other than the cases, keyboards and mice. Dead hard drives with the covers removed make attractive display items, but there's no reason to go nuts with a macabre display of damaged parts unless you are teaching computer assembly or repair.

Different case manufacturers ship their products with different accessory packs, which means that you'll often be short a few screws of one type or another doing a build. Here comes the most valuable piece of advice I can give an aspiring PC builder. Don't keep all your extra screws in one box! There are three basic screw sizes used in assembling PCs, so do yourself a big favor and start with three boxes for spare screws from Day One. I once caught myself spending a minute apiece searching for hard drive screws in the all-inclusive box a predecessor had started. I got so angry that I went out to an industrial fastener place and bought a couple thousand. It was well worth it. Another bit of advice is to put the plastic or rubber feet on the case as soon as you start the build, or you're likely to forget. Aside from that, I would suggest McGraw-Hill's "Build Your Own PC" series by Morris Rosenthal (shameless self-promotion) for standard building techniques.

One question that often comes up is whether by building a PC from all FCC Class B (residential use) parts you end up with a PC that is FCC Class B certified. The answer is "No." You don't even end up with a PC that is FCC Class A (business use) certified. For a PC to receive FCC certification, it has to be submitted to a FCC test suite, configured as it will be sold. I believe they give manufacturers some latitude when it comes to building essentially identical PCs, providing the manufacturer does RF emissions testing on their own, something you need a real lab to do. All of this doesn't mean that your home built PCs wouldn't pass the FCC Class B certification if they were tested, it just means that you shouldn't legally represent them as such.

Assembling from Bare-Bones

One reason many PC shops assemble their finished PCs from bare-bones base systems is to get that FCC sticker on the case. A bare bones system is usually defined as a case, power supply, motherboard, and memory, though it often includes a video card or a floppy drive as well. In other words, the system is already built to the point where it could be sent out for FCC testing. The real advantage to buying bare-bones systems is that it simplifies troubleshooting and warranty returns. If you can't get the system to boot with a known good video card, you can just send it back. The downside is that it reduces the art of computer building to screwing in drives and adapters. Another advantage is that you can buy assembled bare bones systems from vendors for less than the cost of the individual parts. Why? Well, for one thing, the labor cost is trivial since it only takes a pro a couple minutes to put together a bare-bones system. It also saves a lot of packing, since the vendor doesn't get their parts in retail packs, and it reduces the vendor's risk that you'll damage the parts during assembly and then want to return them.

Just because bare-bones systems are assembled by somebody who does a lot of them doesn't mean that they do a very good job. It always pays to take a minute and look the system over carefully to make sure they didn't skimp on screws or mount the floppy drive at an angle. It's especially important to check that you are getting what you paid for. I don't know a single vendor who wouldn't honestly believe that they were doing you a favor by making a few "equivalent" trades to get you a system on time. Usually that doesn't matter, but if specific hardware has been specified in a contract or by a customer, why take the chance? Memory is traditionally an area in which vendors fool around and deliver what they have in stock, so don't forget to check the module speed even if it counts up the memory correctly.

Production Line Techniques and Testing

Setting up the "perfect" assembly area is a big waste of time. PC assembly is not automotive production, and you don't have the control over your raw materials that real manufacturers have. At first blush, spending a few hundred dollars on wood and building custom workbenches with a monitor shelf on top might look like a great idea, but it's not. The ideal workspace for computer assembly is a broad flat space with decent lighting and access to a power strip. I wasted a lot of time and not a little money fooling around with custom benches and racking, but you can't beat folding tables from office superstores. Stick with the five-foot or six-foot length. The longer ones get too heavy and won't fit in a hatchback if you want to take them to a show. I like to attach a couple of power strips to the metal rim under the table, though you could mount them right on the table surface if you hate bending your knees.

There's also no reason to install permanent networking infrastructure in your assembly area. A couple of 100BaseT drops hanging from the ceiling with plenty of slack are all you need. The only exception is if you will be using your assembly space for classroom training, in which case you'll want to tie-wrap bundles of network cables to the bottoms of the tables. The most important thing to have easy access to in your assembly area is an Internet connected PC. While most builds shouldn't require you to pop onto the web to download patches, you'll be running your troubleshooting and repair shop in the same space.

I resisted electric screwdrivers for years. I also got lots of pains in my shoulder. I didn't like them because it was just too easy to strip the cheap screws that come with most cases, both on tightening and loosening. The technology has gotten better, with clutches and torque control, so I'd consider a high quality rechargeable screwdriver a reasonable investment. I still stick with manual screwdrivers on service calls, where the risk outweighs the convenience. Besides, if my batteries wear down I can always eat a candy bar or drink some coffee.

"Burn-in" is no longer as widely hyped as it once was, and it was never such a well defined quantity anyway. Most bids require a "24 hour burn-in" without specifying any further, and most computer builders cheat. This isn't as terrible as it sounds, since if the PC boots and doesn't lock-up during the Windows installation process, it's pretty well tested. Burn-in is far more important for mass manufacturers who have the pre-configured operating system pre-installed on the hard drive, and therefore do not exercise any of the components in a particular PC except through some sort of burn-in process. When I was in the hardware business, I actually did do 24 hour burn-ins, using CheckIt to beat the snot out of the drives and memory for the whole 24 hours. This ruined a lot of floppy disks and probably a couple of floppy drives with no real benefit. The main advantage of burn-in was to catch improperly connected serial and parallel ports, but these are all mounted on the motherboards now. On rare, rare occasions, Checkit might have saved me a service call for a hard drive that failed butterfly reads or memory that dropped a bit in the 23rd hour, maybe two instances of each in thousands of PCs built. If you consider the cost of electricity to run all those machines for 24 hours, not to mention the space it took up, it probably would have been more cost effective to skip it. These days, if I want to give a machine a burn-in, I just run a Windows screen saver overnight. If it hasn't locked up by morning, and if you can shut down Windows and reboot a couple seconds later, it's as good a test as any.

⚓ INFRASTRUCTURE

Working Out of the House

Looking back over a lifetime of handing out unsolicited advice, I think that the worst steer I ever gave somebody was pushing a friend with whom I'd built a successful small computer company (over a million dollars a year sales) to move out of his house and into commercial space. I had three real motivations for doing this, two of which had nothing to do with conducting business. His house was on a nice, quiet, residential street, and although the neighbors weren't complaining (at least to me), I felt bad about the increasing truck traffic, especially when a common carrier (semi-trailer) delivered a large order, taking down a neighbor's low hanging tree branch. Second, it drove me nuts that he always parked near his front door, effectively blocking the driveway and forcing everybody else to park in front of the houses of his neighbors. Depending on what was going on, this could be a half-dozen or more cars, and some idiot would usually try to pull into the end of the driveway and block the sidewalk. If I had lived on the street, I would have complained to the city. Finally, I worried about how it affected our credibility with customers. One day, a potential big customer from a state agency came with a couple people to look us over, and from their body language, it was clear that we had just lost the business. I suppose I felt bad about the mountains of trash we put out on garbage day too.

Well, the hell with the occasional missed opportunity, and the truth is, we could have rented a conference room in one of the virtual office facilities that exist in every major city, just to give people just like us a prestigious address. The neighbors weren't complaining, so most of the problem was probably in my head. Working out of the home offers so many financial advantages and creature comforts that I consider it the first option for anybody who isn't opening a retail store. The primary financial advantage of working out of the home is that you're already paying for it. Security is less of a worry since you sleep there. You have a full kitchen and bathrooms, not to mention an extra phone line (your house phone) at no extra cost. You don't have to worry about negotiating or understanding commercial rental agreements, which generally commit you to a minimum of a full year.

There are some downsides however. First there is the little matter of zoning. If you live in an area that is zoned residential, you are somewhat at the mercy of your neighbors. There are businesses that can be legally conducted in most residential neighborhoods, but the rules usually preclude employees, manufacturing, and anything else that might impact the quality of life in the area. From the standpoint of carrying out a computer business, lack of open space is one of the biggest drawbacks to working out of the home. Unless you are willing to trash all your furniture and convert the whole ground floor into a computer workshop, you'll always be tripping over boxes and searching for an open space just to set something down. Power can be a problem also, if you're building and testing lots of computers. The standard 15 amp breakers in most homes will have you running extension cords all over the place to spread the load. Finally, of course, there is the credibility issue with people who want to see your manufacturing facility, but that does bring up a key business rule. It's not the quantity of customers that's important, it's how they fit into your business operations. If it costs you $20K a year in rent to add a single, large customer who is expected to bring you $20K a year in profit, you're working for free. The worst drawback of paying for commercial space is that it brings about accelerated attempts to raise revenue to justify the expense. This leads to making poor hires, selling at low margins, and gambling on businesses outside of your core competency.

Rented/Owned Commercial Space

The biggest single expense a computer business is likely to generate, after employee salaries, is renting commercial space. Commercial space in the US is rented one of two ways: either a monthly rent figure (common for office space), or per square foot per year (frequently retail and industrial space). A 1000 square foot retail space advertised for $10/sf will cost $10K a year, before add-ons. Renting commercial property is appreciably trickier than renting an apartment, and you better read your lease carefully. I once took a job with a company that had been renting an overpriced, undersized place for almost two years, and was considering a move. I read their lease, and it turned out that by not giving notice a few months earlier, they had committed to continuing the lease for three additional years! Some commercial landlords and holding companies are famous for being a little slippery, so read everything, and if you don't understand the terms, don't sign. Among other clauses that work against you, many landlords try to get you to agree to built in rent increases, as much as $1/sf per year, on the theory that they are cutting you a break on your first year. You might figure you're going to move soon anyway but moving a business is far more expensive than you might think. Aside from the interruption of operations, there's the reworking of the phones and network, the address change on business cards and stationery, contacting anyone who needs to know that you've moved, it all adds up.

Most commercial space is rented as "triple net," a coded way of saying that you're on the hook for the property taxes, along with insurance for the building, maintenance and all other operating expenses. Make sure you understand who pays for the light bulbs, snow removal and landscaping before you sign a lease. If a flood carries the building off, you may still be expected to mail the landlord a check every month. A "double net" lease commits you to pay for the same as triple-net, but the landlord is responsible for the walls, the roof and the floor. In a "single net" lease, you pay the rent and sometimes, depending on the terms, part of the above expenses. You'll still have to obtain business insurance for your contents and liability. Whatever amount of time and money you estimate it will take you to move into commercial property, double it and hope that you get off so cheap.

Special Development Zones and Incubators

There is a third option that falls somewhere between working out of your house and entering the cold, cruel world of commercial real estate. Welcome to the world of government subsidies. You really need to do your homework, both via the Internet

Sunny - Occasional Meteor Showers

and by visiting local government offices from City Hall to the
state unemployment agency, to make sure you aren't missing an
opportunity. There are three major reasons for the government
to make subsidized real estate available to local businesses. The
first is pork barrel politics. Bringing home some money to support local business is always a vote getter on election day for the
local congressman or state representative who has some pull in
their respective legislature. These efforts are sometimes charac-
terized by lack of focus or ridiculous goals.

The second type of subsidy involves the establishment of special development zones in otherwise unattractive locations.
Establishing a business in one of these zones may result in tax
relief or actual cash subsidies towards employee wages or rent.
Most of these special zones are set up in poor neighborhoods
with bad infrastructure and crime problems, and their intent is
social engineering, as opposed to unfettered capitalism. It may be
difficult to get employees to come to these neighborhoods, likewise customers for retail operations. However, these zones are
sometimes established in commercial areas that have been losing
business tenants for other reasons, and may be ideal for you.

The final type of subsidy is the incubator, often sponsored
by local government with some support from the business community. Incubators are generally established in some large space
nobody can figure out what to do with, like old mills, un-
rented sky-scrapers or abandoned factories. They attempt to
offer something of a mother-hen service to new businesses.
Incubators are often intended to bring a certain type of business
to the area, such as high-tech, so you may have to tweak your
business plan (or make one up) to get in. The rent at incubators isn't always cheap, though the leases should be friendlier
than what you'll encounter in the real world. Incubators offer
other advantages such as: a conference room for meeting cus-

tomers, free or subsidized secretarial services, high speed Internet access, access to free or subsidized business consulting services, even a cafeteria. One drawback with incubators is that they may lead participants into making heavy expenditures, as the incubator staff and consultants may be wholly lacking in genuine small business experience. Never be quick about taking business advice from somebody who hasn't risked their own savings in a business. The National Business Incubation Association lists member incubators across the country at www.nbia.org/links/index.php.

On the similar subject, if you establish a woman or minority owned company, you have an advantage bidding on government contracts and on subcontracts with companies which do a lot of government business that include set-asides for woman and minority owned companies. We should mention that there are also some government funded loan guarantees available for woman and minority owned businesses.

Phone, Internet, Utilities, Vehicle

The main difference between a business and a residential phone is that a business line costs more and includes a Yellow Pages listing. You can buy cheap two-line phones that will work with any home lines and allow you to put people on hold. Having two phone lines available is a necessity, particularly if your Internet connection is dial-up. Serious multi-line phone systems require a PBX (Private Branch Exchange), cost thousands of dollars and are a pain to set up. Don't even consider going this route unless you have a half-dozen full-time employees working in an office environment. There are also inexpensive roll-over switches that will allow you to run a three line phone system without investing in a PBX, but it makes less and less sense to invest in phone infrastructure as increasingly attractive cellular phone deals are becoming available.

Speakerphones can be dangerous. A company I worked for once submitted a bid for several million dollars worth of hardware on a state contract for which we were a favored vendor. It was a bigger deal than we could have directly financed, but an OEM with whom we had done well over a million dollars of business was willing to finance the deal for us. They sent us a final price for the PCs, which was incredibly aggressive, we added our markup and submitted the bid to the state office. A few hours later, I received a frantic call from the OEM, saying they had left the monitors out of the price quote! They knew we had already submitted the bid, so they turned their suppliers upside down for prices on the cheapest possible hardware that could be stretched to meet the bid spec. If we cut our profit margin in half and used the junk they were offering, we could hold the price we had submitted. I sat with the salesman who had bid the contract as he called the customer to inform them of the changes and say we could still meet the price. The call was placed on speakerphone, but we only got through to the customer's voice mail. We then proceeded to enter into a conversation about the bid, using language I'd like to characterize as colorful, but frankly, it was just crude. The discussion got pretty ugly, as I made clear exactly why I felt the stuff the OEM wanted us to bid was garbage. Suddenly, the speakerphone intoned, "If you wish to submit your message, press 1". If you wish to review your message, press 2", . . . " The phone line had been open the whole time, and our whole conversation had been recorded! I yelled something like, "Hit 2, edit the message," but the salesman panicked and hung up. To this day, there's probably a copy of the recording floating around a state purchasing office.

The level of Internet access you need depends entirely on what type of business you end up running. If you only use the Internet for e-mail and downloading drivers and software patches, you can certainly get by with dial-up. As soon as you go beyond that – designing websites for customers, purchasing online, or even trying to start your own retail site – you better sign up for high speed, always-on access of one kind or another. If you have a home office and already have cable TV installed, a cable modem is an easy upgrade route, provided your local cable company offers the service. The other practical option is a DSL line, either purchased directly through your local phone carrier, or through a package deal with a national service like AOL. Both of these services are sold with contracts that preclude you from reselling Internet access to others. If you want to have your own server online, the best solution is to rent a spot at a co-location facility, which will probably cost you a couple hundred dollars a month. See: www.colosource.com/findacolo.asp.

Your main utility bill will either be phone or electricity, though depending on your heating system and location, you could get a pretty stiff bill in the winter as well. Water is generally a small expense, and may even be paid by the landlord if you're renting. The phone bill is largely dependent on your long distance carrier and how you conduct business (i.e. how much time you spend making phone calls, how much you use your cell phone). If you are paying more than five cents a minute for long distance, you're paying too much. Often it will make sense to make your outgoing calls on a cell phone if it includes a bundle of free long distance minutes in the basic monthly bill. These penny pinching decisions that save you a few cents a minute are likely to save you a few dollars a day, which can add up to over $1000 a year, and if that's not real money to you, you're reading the wrong book.

When you go into business, there's a good chance you already own a car, and I strongly advise trying to get by without a dedicated business vehicle. It's cheap to add business coverage to your personal car insurance to cover delivery activity, and you can always rent a van or hire a delivery service for large deliveries. You aren't a plumber or an electrician, and nobody is going to call you to set up a corporate network because they saw your name artfully and expensively painted on the side of a van. A magnetic sign is inexpensive and easily transferred from vehicle to vehicle. The federal government allows you a tax deduction of over thirty cents a mile for business use of your vehicle, so unless you drive a gas-guzzler, you can actually break even on driving it. As soon as you buy or lease a van specifically for business use, you incur a huge expense that doesn't earn you any money, plus a big insurance bill. Sure it's a deduction, but we'll explain why deductions don't offset expenses in the next chapter.

Office Equipment, Demo Hardware, LAN

The first temptation on setting up a new business, whether in the home or in a commercial space, is to stock up on "necessary" office equipment. From my experiences, the only equipment you really need to get started is a phone, a fax, an internet connected computer and a printer. If you're going to do any web design work, then a $50 scanner is a good idea too, but that's really about it. Whatever furniture you are already using to support your computer is good enough to be your business desk, and a couple of cardboard boxes are as good a place as any to start a filing system. A $5 plastic multi-tray correspondence unit is also nice for providing temporary storage for open issues like bills, customer invoices, merchandise quotes and sales proposals. If you really feel the need to buy a piece of furniture, I'd start with that five or six-foot folding table from Staples and a table cloth to cover it for classy demos. What you don't need is a copying machine, not even a cheap one, and definitely not a lease. Forget about executive desks, rows of filing cabinets, and tilt & swivel chairs. You're trying to build a computer business, not a giant dollhouse for "Business Barbie."

One of the big expenses in the computer business used to be demo hardware. Salesmen always like having the actual unit they are trying to sell available for the customer to fool around with. Unfortunately, this immediately lowers the value of that hardware which can no longer be sold as new, and it loses additional value as it ages with every passing day. Now, the truth of the situation, as proved by Dell, Gateway and others, is you don't need demo equipment to sell hardware. Your customers have seen PCs before, it's not a thrill. The most successful retail computer stores feature long glass display cases of motherboards, behind which a somewhat knowledgeable salesperson takes orders for custom PCs, bringing out any other parts the customer asks about, like an old-fashioned butcher displaying cuts of beef. The only place where demo systems make sense is in superstores and other mass-merchandisers who have dozens of each particular model of the brand-name PCs they are displaying stacked out back.

The one situation in which you will need to make an investment in PC hardware is if you provide training classes. Whether you have a retail location or rent space from an office center on an "as-needed" basis, it helps smooth things out if you have a collection of identical machines for your classroom. This vastly simplifies software installation and troubleshooting, not to mention eliminating computer envy, as in "How come HE always gets the good monitor." If you build the systems in mini-towers and use flat LCD displays, you can easily fit eight complete systems in an economy car. Just don't leave it unattended unless you have great insurance. Most training environments require a LAN, which you can easily implement with 100BaseT and cabling and a $100 hub. Don't go overboard in rented space installing permanent 100BaseT infrastructure, with in-wall cabling and a wire closet, unless you can get it knocked off the rent. Better to use some cheap stick-on molding to hide the cables and save a couple hundred dollars worth of parts and a couple thousand dollars worth of time (your time isn't free anymore).

Subcontractors

Employees are a problem. My take on employees in computer start-ups of any kind is that about half of the employees will actually cost your business money during every hour they "work," while the other half make money. If you're lucky, the half that make money will work more than 40 hours a week while the other half will sneak out early every day, so the net will be positive. Many small businesses try to limit their expenses and tax filing requirements by hiring any help as independent contractors, also known as 1099's, for the tax form you report their earnings on. Actually, you can pay independent contractors up to $600 a year without having to issue a 1099 and still take the tax write-off, but you can't get a whole lot of work for $600. The government has a whole set of guidelines as to who is and isn't an independent contractor, Publication 1779, available online at www.irs.gov/pub/irs-pdf/p1779.pdf.

It's not a simple matter of what you and the person doing the work find the most convenient and, if you abuse the system, you could end up facing lots of back taxes, penalties, and interest.

Used properly, subcontractors can lower your direct costs, your overhead and your headaches. If you hire subcontractors who have been self-employed for some time, you probably don't have to worry about responsibility issues. It's nearly impossible for somebody to be chronically irresponsible and to make a go of it being self-employed. Assuming the subcontractors you hire are competent in their areas of expertise, it also removes the overhead you would invest in training employees. One of the greatest advantages of using subcontractors is that they come without baggage. They pretend no loyalty to you and demand none in return. If you have work for them, great. If not, they don't expect to be paid to sit around drinking coffee. The main thing you have to watch out for is retaining subcontractors who are new to being self-employed and don't understand the increased tax liabilities they are taking on.

🚢 ACCOUNTING

The Truth about Write-Offs

Everybody who's not in business and knows somebody who is, has heard of that wonderful thing called a write-off. Maybe a friend has treated you to lunch or paid the tolls on a road, with a wink and a "it's a write-off." Maybe you've already talked to an accountant who's told you about saving all your receipts so they can be written-off. Write-offs work like this: when you file your taxes at the end of the year, you get to subtract your business expenses from your business income. INCOME. So, for starters, you need to be making money to benefit from write-offs. Many business expenses are unavoidable, but here we're applying the term "write-off" to purchases you didn't absolutely require. We're going to use some round numbers and generalizations in the following paragraphs for the sake of illustration. Income tax rates change frequently, and taxes are highly dependent on an individual's situation in life, number of children, etc. . . . However, the principles illustrated by these examples hold; it's just the percentages that may change. The discussion gets a little complicated, but we sum it up in a table at the end.

Now, take the example used in **Setting Prices** of a first year in business where you do $200,000 in gross sales your first year and end up with a gross profit of $28,000. In that example, I allowed you $8000 for non-critical expenses (which were already figured in). Keep in mind that by spending this money on allowable deductions, you no longer have it in your pocket. It's gone. So you reduced your net profits from $28,000 to $20,000, but what does that save you? Self-employed people are subject to self-employment tax, in which you make the Social Security and Medicare payments that are deducted from all workers' paychecks (yours in this case), plus you make the employer's matching contribution. This runs around 15.3%, meaning that by reducing your self-employed income by $8,000, you already saved $1,224 on your taxes. Your total self-employment tax payment is $3,060. This does come at the price that your eventual Social Security benefits will be lower, since you contributed less. You do get to deduct half of that self-employment tax from your income, and between that and the standard deductions, your taxable federal income will be down under $12,000. Let's say you are living on the cheap and you make a $2,000 IRA contribution (also money out of your pocket), and your taxable income is down to $8,970. You pay the 15% marginal rate on that income (2001 tax year rate), which means your income tax bill is $1,345, and your total Federal Tax bill is around $4,405. Pay another $449 in state or city tax (5% for our example), and you have a total tax bill of $4,854 and an after tax (and voluntary IRA contribution) income of around $15,146.

Now let's say you had no business write-offs, keeping in mind that merchandise you buy and sell (inventory) is not a write-off. You would have paid 15.3% self-employment tax on $28,000, or $4284. You would then have paid income tax

(same $2,000 IRA contribution and deductions) on around
$16,358 at the same 15% marginal rate for a $2,456 Federal
Income tax bill, and a total Federal Tax bill of $6,738. Your
state tax will have crept up a few hundred dollars to $817,and
your total tax liability on the year is $7,557. Strangely enough,
that leaves you with $20,443 in pocket money. So, generating
$8000 in write-offs saved you over $2,500 on your tax bill, but
you ended up with $5,297 less in your pocket and a decreased
Social Security benefit. What happened?

That $8,000 you spent on flying to the PC show in Vegas, a
new tilt-and-swivel leather chair, and the notebook with the

Net profit (Schedule C) after required expenses	$28,000	$28,000
Unnecessary expenses (Write-Offs)	$8.000	0
Net Income for Self Employment Tax (SE) and Income Tax (1040)	$20,000 (15.3% tax=$3,060)	$28,000 (15.3% tax=$4,284)
1/2 Self Employment tax	$1,530	$2,142
IRA Contribution	$2,000	$2,000
Standard Deductions (approx.)	$7.500	$7.500
Taxable Income	$8,970	$16,358
Federal Income Tax (2001 year)	$1.345 (15% bracket)	$2.456 (15% bracket)
Income Tax + Self Employed Tax	$4,405	$6,740
State Tax (depends on state)	$449 (5% for example)	$817 (5% for example)
Total Taxes	$4,854	$7,557
After Tax Earnings	$15,146	$20,443

15" LCD, is gone. You don't have it anymore. The good side is, not having it, you don't have to pay taxes on it. The bad side is, not having it, you really don't have it. What you've essentially done is purchased those things you wrote-off at a discount. That discount, ignoring again the marginal drop in Social Security benefits, is the $2,703 you save on your tax bill divided by the $8000 you spent, or 34%. Basically, that discount remains constant until you push your income into the next tax bracket, for which you'll need to sell quite a few more computers. Again, the only way to earn that discount is to buy stuff, which means the money is gone!

Retirement Saving

In the previous tax example, we used a $2,000 IRA deduction to lower your income tax burden. You should put the maximum amount of money you can into retirement plans because along with reducing your taxes, the money remains yours. Social Security is an insurance program, not a savings plan. Your Social Security benefit depends on politics, amongst other factors, and if you die, you lose, you can't give your Social Security benefits away in your will. Individual Retirement Accounts (IRA's) belong to you. You can invest the money almost anyway you like and if you need it before you retire, you can withdraw it, though you'll have to pay a penalty in many cases. The standard IRA contribution has been raised to $3,000 through 2004, after which it jumps to $4,000 in 2005 and $5,000 in 2008. You should talk about the advantages and disadvantages of the different types of IRAs with the investment institution you choose to set up with.

In addition to a regular IRA, there are other tax-exempt savings plans available to self-employed individuals, and as of

2002, this includes 401K's!. I have a Self Employed Pension Plan (SEP) which allows me to contribute up to 15% of my income, sheltering that money from income tax (as with the IRA, it doesn't help any with self-employment tax). It follows a crazy formula I always forget, which is why I'm putting in the book so I'll know where to find it. The allowable contribution is computed from three factors:

A = Net earnings from Schedule C

B = Deduction for self employment
(one half of amount paid)

C = The Factor =
(contribution percentage) / (1 + contribution percentage)

At a contribution percentage of 15%

C = 0.15/1.15 = 0.1304

Contribution = (A-B)*C

Using our tax example above, our small business gets an additional tax deduction of

(20,000-1,530)*0.1304 =
$2,408 when taking $8,000 in write-offs,

Or , (28,000-2,142) * 0,1304 = $3,372.

In both cases, the SEP contribution will lower your taxes, but in the latter case, you get to deduct almost $1,000 more from your taxable income, in return for increasing your retirement savings! The SEP limit is being raised from 15% to 25% in 2002, though according to our formula, the practical limit for a sole proprietor is 20%. Reducing taxes through saving money makes a lot more sense to me than buying an alligator skin notebook or some other unnecessary business accessory.

Business Tax Schedules

If you've absolutely never filed your own taxes before, this discussion will strike you as starting in the middle, since I only intend to address the business related sections of the Income Tax. You should be familiar with the basic information on the Form 1040 (the mother of all tax forms) before reading this discussion. The four basic forms the sole proprietor will encounter are the Schedule C (Profit or Loss From Business), Schedule SE (Self Employment), Form 4562 (Depreciation and Amortization) and Form 8829 (Business Use of the Home). Schedule SE depends on Schedule C, which itself depends on Forms 4562 and 8829, so we'll go in the order you have to take when you actually file your taxes. For the record, I'm not trying to advise you on how to deal with your specific tax return here, and I sure don't want to get sued for giving bad advice. If you aren't comfortable filing your own taxes, hire an accountant, and pay for an extra hour to go over the return with the accountant when it's finished. The only goal here is to give you an idea of how taxes affect your overall business. The IRS has invaluable information for starting a new business at www.irs.gov. You need to navigate through the site from the options list on the left side of the page, first "business" and then "small business." The regional office of your state Department of Revenue (taxman) will often offer free courses for new businesses, which tend to focus on tax issues.

Form 4562 (Depreciation and Amortization) is the most intimidating form for the uninitiated, due to the high level of accounting jargon involved in depreciating assets. Depreciation describes how you write-off the value of an asset, say an automobile or a lathe, which has a long useful life. The IRS has whole laundry lists of which items should be depreciated over what time period, but the saving grace for most small business owners is the ability to expense certain property (i.e., take the whole value in a single year). The maximum dollar limitation for expensing property in 2001 is $24,000, which is more than enough to cover all of the assets a small business will acquire in a year. However, if your income is so low your first year in business that you don't owe much (or any) income tax, depreciating that new office computer and laser printer may make more sense than expensing it. Depreciating property over a period of years requires some pretty careful record keeping, but it does allow you to move some of the cost into a future year, when you might be paying income tax in a higher bracket and the deduction will be worth more. Since I've never owned any business real-estate or purchased a vehicle for the business, I don't think I've ever spent more than $5,000 on business property in a year, and I've always elected to expense the full amount in that year. In the end, it only takes me about ten minutes to fill out 4562, and half of that is spent on doing the auto mileage deduction on the back of the form. If you don't buy any business property (other than supplies which go on the Schedule C), you don't have to file a 4562 and can take your car mileage on the back of Schedule C.

Form 8829 (Business Use of the Home) is pretty self explanatory, as far as tax forms go, but you'll want to look over publication 587 before filing. This particular publication is highly readable and contains an example of how Schedule C and Forms 4562 and 8829 are filled out. You can only get this deduction for the part of your home that you use regularly and exclusively for the business. Your home can be a home that you own (either outright or paying a mortgage) or a house or apartment that you rent. I would definitely recommend talking to an accountant before you start fooling around with "Depreciation of Your Home," because you could end up with quite a tax headache when you or your heirs eventually sell the house. The basic approach for arriving at what percentage of your expenses are deductible is to divide the area (in square feet) you use for the business by the area of the whole home. You then add up all the listed home expenses (rent is a "line 20 – other expense") and get to take that percentage as a deduction.

Schedule C, Profit or Loss from Business, is the heart of the business filing. The big ticket items on this schedule are "gross receipts or sales" (how much money the business brought in), and "cost of goods sold" (the cost of the merchandise you bought for resale, both raw materials and finished products). The "cost of goods sold" has its own special section on the back of Schedule C where you account for inventory, materials, labor, and new purchases minus items withdrawn for personal use. The main issue here is inventory. You add together the value of the inventory you had at the end of the previous year with the inventory costs incurred in the current year, then subtract the value of the inventory at the end of the current year. This gives you the cost of goods sold for the current year. The problem in the computer business is that the value of inventory is constantly dropping, so the CPU that cost you $400 last year and sat on your shelf all this year without being sold may be worth nothing at the end of the current year. If you use the "lower of cost or market" method, you end up writing off that CPU when you value it at zero in your end of the year inventory. When you change the value of items in inventory from a previously declared value, you have to include a note to explain the change.

I've always been able to file the short form on Schedule SE, but both the short and long form are on the same physical sheet of paper. A little flow chart on the top half of the page tells you which form (which side of the sheet) you'll have to file. The long form is primarily used by farmers and clergy. The key part of Schedule SE is that you have to bring over your net profit (or loss) from your completed Schedule C, and multiply by 0.9235. If the result is less than $400, you don't owe self employment tax. In 2001, as a sole proprietor, your actual self employment tax was 15.3% of your net profit (up to $80,400). After $80,400, you still pay the medical part, but not the straight social security. Once you've computed the self employment tax, you get to use half that amount as an income tax deduction on the front of the 1040.

Manual Accounting vs. Software

Your bookkeeping requirements are driven by what kind of business you are in and how the business is structured. Most of this book is focused on the sole proprietor, but we'll talk a little about incorporation later on. Corporations require both a higher standard of bookkeeping and, if you're looking for bank loans, audits by a CPA (Certified Public Accountant). When you start out in business, you have two basic choices. You can do your bookkeeping on paper, using the checkbook register from a business bank account, or you can use business accounting software from the very first day. Both approaches have their advantages, but I'll make the argument for the paper approach first.

Paper and pen are simply more "real" to me than filling in the blanks on a computer screen, and the last thing you want to do as a new business is lose touch with reality. Remember the real estate crash of the late-Eighties? My theory is that it was due, in large part, to the invention of the spreadsheet. Once you set up a spreadsheet formula that accounts for the basic expenses arising from construction, taxes, land, etc. . . . , you can forget about the very real factors that went into that formula and start playing with numbers. Assume a $12/sf rent, you break even. $14/sf, you make money. Hey, $16/sf, you're cleaning up. What a fun game, and even the banks fell for it. The problem wasn't with the formulas, it was with the assumptions they hid from the users who started believing that the game was real. Just because you stick a number in one end and get millions in profits coming out the other doesn't make it real, as everybody soon found out. If you've been in business before, it will probably save you a little time to put your whole business on disk from the inception, but if you're a first timer, I believe that the checkbook register will help you keep your feet on the ground. If and when business picks up to the point that a software accounting package offers a real labor savings, you can always cut over to one at the cost of a few hours of data entry on a weekend. All accounting software requires at least a little time to master, while the checkbook register is a marvel of simplicity.

The advantage of software bookkeeping systems is that they automate many of the tasks you would otherwise have to do manually, such as math. Most packages also feature automatic check printing for expenses entered into the system, or online payment (electronic money transfer) for vendors who support it. Other features include creating invoices, payroll and tax preparation, with the help of an inexpensive add-on. If you form a corporation, by working with a software package your accountant supports, you'll save the accountant's time (and your money) on preparing your corporate filings. Some packages also feature inventory control, but beware that this can lull you into the false sense of security that you're in control of the inventory you shouldn't even have! Of course, all these business accounting packages cost money, from under a hundred bucks, to a couple thousand for a networked business version. I've talked the whole thing over with my brother-in-law, who is a CPA with no particular axe to grind, and his take was that QuickBooks is the best bet for a small business with no special requirements. They have a new version that lets you process credit cards online without buying a card-swiper, which could save you $500, and you can also outsource your payroll through them.

There is an intermediate step, between running the whole business out of the checkbook register and a fully integrated bookkeeping system, which is a mix of elements. There are super cheap software packages, under twenty dollars, that will print and track invoices, and some that will even track inventory. For those of you who like fooling around with spreadsheets, you can certainly set up some templates for invoicing, and also for pricing systems. I've been using the same DOS based invoicing software, "My Invoices", since 1994 for my consulting business. It's so simple and effective that I've had no motivation to change. I think it cost me ten dollars.

Whether you go all manual, all computerized, or a mix of these elements, it's critical that you properly categorize your income and expenses. There is always the temptation to label both expenses and sales as simply as possible, such as "hardware" or "service." Sure, it fits easily into the checkbook register or saves time setting up categories in software, but by the end of the year you won't know what these items really mean without digging through your paper invoices to find out. Unless you have a photographic memory, it means you'll be losing insight into what specific areas of your business are really clicking and which are a drag on profits. Don't worry about creating too many categories. You can always assign them to a smaller number of overarching groups.

Let me venture a final warning about accounting software and bookkeepers. I once worked in a small company with a couple million in sales, mounting losses, and a full-time bookkeeper who "worked damned hard" and didn't have a clue what was wrong with the company. The last thing a small business that's losing money needs is more bookkeepers and business consultants. I've seen more businesses fail from the overhead of carrying deadweight employees and consultants than any other reason. Don't get fooled into thinking that bookkeeping is some black art that you can never master. Hire a bookkeeper when you're making so much money that you're having a hard time keeping track of it, not when you don't even have a profit.

Accountants and Tax Preparers

I usually like accountants, for a couple of reasons. First, I've never met one who was a "Yes" man. When your business is losing money, your CPA will tell you, "Your business is losing money." Maybe it's a lack of imagination, but no, when it comes to explaining things to the IRS (and shareholders, in the case of public companies), accountants can be very imaginative. The primary function of a CPA is not to keep your books for you, that's your job. The two real jobs of the CPA are to handle corporate filings and to save you money on taxes. While a CPA is not generally a tax lawyer, they are responsible for interpreting the tax code, hopefully in such a way as to save you money. The simpler your business is, the less benefit you derive from hiring a CPA to do your taxes.

Paid tax preparers, on the other hand, are usually people just like you who went through a course on tax preparation and may have less business experience than you do. Since running a tax efficient business requires you to have a thorough knowl-

FINDING AN ACCOUNTANT

edge of how deductions actually work, I think the practice of hiring anybody other than an accountant to do your taxes is just laziness. If you do the taxes yourself, at least your first year in business, you'll learn what it means to run a tax efficient business. If you don't want to do your taxes yourself, study the return the accountant files for you and pay for an extra hour of his or her time to sit down and explain anything that doesn't strike you as obvious. Taxes and business are inseparable. If you don't understand what's going on with your taxes, you can't understand what's going on with your business.

Insurance and Other Necessary Evils

What's so bad about insurance? Well, it's like gambling against the house, and letting the casino change the rules for your next visit in case you win. There are two types of insurance you can buy. The first is for your own peace of mind, the second is to fulfill business or legal requirements. Examples of the first are things like life insurance. I don't have any life insurance, or health insurance for that matter, and I don't worry about it. Not because I'm an idiot, but because I couldn't have made it during the years I was working to develop a business and become a writer if I had bought health insurance. It literally would have broke me. If I was married, I would buy all the term life I was allowed to. I think a big term life policy beats roses and chocolates as a way of saying "I Love You," but maybe that's why I'm still single.

The second type of insurance is the kind you are required to purchase by law or by contractual obligations. For example, auto insurance is required by law in most states, and banks require mortgage holders to buy homeowners insurance. Many customers, particularly corporations and government agencies, won't let you on site without liability insurance to protect them from your claims of being injured while working on their site. If your payroll is large enough, you might be required to provide employee health insurance. Partners may require each other to get life insurance or business continuation insurance policies to protect the business in case of death or disability, and if you want to cover your business assets against theft or damage, you'll need a business policy, or a rider on your home insurance. Basically, you can insure yourself for any eventuality, including the sun going nova, but it's all a gamble against the odds.

If you have employees, the government mandates that you buy workers compensation insurance. Workers comp is charged on a per employee basis, as a percentage of the employees pay. The percentage, or multiplier, can be as high as 40% for some occupations, such as roofing, where the cost per accident is understandably high. In a computer business, the most expensive employees are those defined as "warehouse," and the insurance adjuster might include your receptionist in "warehouse" if she fills shipping and receiving functions. On the bright side, workers comp costs have dropped more than 50% in my home state of Massachusetts since 1993, and better controls have been bringing costs down across the country. Workers comp will amount to at least a couple percent of your payroll, and I think it's possible to get retroactively nailed if you cheat on the number of employees covered, though many small businesses do. It's one of the leading reasons small businesses try to use 1099 employees or subcontract other corporations rather than making regular hires. I wrote the following ditty when I was working for a company that had just been handed a big worker's comp bill, despite being on the way to bankruptcy.

Workers Comp

Our business has been treated cruelly
So let this note inform you duly
We let go all our warehouse staff
Workers comp's at fault, don't laugh
The secretary, techs, all lost
So please take note, adjust our cost
Our showroom's closed, we're in a tailspin
There's one guy left, and he's a salesman.

Is Cash King?

Many small businessmen will tell you "Cash is King" and they
will even give customers discounts for paying in cash. The word
"cash" has two possible meanings. There is the hard cash, as in
the famous $100 bill, and there is cash on delivery, which
means: payment now, rather than on terms. In both cases, you
can take the money to the bank, put it in your business account
and do more business with it. Since obtaining money to do
business normally costs you money (in the way of interest), it's
pretty obvious why getting paid up front can merit a small discount. However, dealing in hard cash is often just an illegal way
to avoid paying taxes. Even if you get away with it, it means the
value of your business will be diminished in the eyes of potential purchasers, to whom you have no way of explaining that
half the income is under the table.

Doing business on the net terms we talked about earlier is
pretty much a necessity with business customers. I've even
heard of some Fortune 500 companies so desperate to show
lower expenses in their current quarter, that they put all of their
suppliers on Net 90, three month payment. This is absolutely
crazy, and not only because it far exceeds any reasonable

amount of time required to process payments. It also limits the number of suppliers who will be willing to do business with those companies, which reduces competition and raises costs. I've done business with cites and towns who were "slow pays" and some who were "fast pays." When dealing with any large organization or bureaucracy, it's critical to invest the time in learning how their payment system works. If you don't submit the proper paperwork, you don't get paid. It might take a month or two for somebody to call you or mail the invoice back with a note that something is wrong. Bureaucracies are usually run by a low-level clerk or secretary who can expedite your payments and make your life much easier if you stay on his or her good side.

Incorporation vs. Sole Proprietorship

Almost all regulations and licenses pertaining to the legal status of your business are handled on the state level. There are a number of differences from state to state in terms of what business forms are recognized, how they are taxed on the-state level, and what fees and paperwork are required. The two most common forms of business for a computer entrepreneur are "S" corporations and sole proprietorships. Partnerships are somewhat more complicated to set up, not from the business form or tax perspective, but due to the basic legal agreement establishing the ground rules of the partnership. If you are going the partnership route, do yourself a favor and consult with a decent business lawyer. Any time you seek professional advice from somebody who charges by the hour, it's absolutely critical that you have your ducks lined up before you go in to talk to them. Don't take the attitude that as the "customer" you can relax and let them do your homework for you. A lawyer will love to fill you in on the basics of doing business in your state and you'll get charged a couple hundred dollars an hour for a lesson you could have gotten out of a $20 book. The following brief descriptions should help you get a handle on the questions you need to ask a lawyer or an accountant, but I recommend buying and studying a book written specifically for how to run a small business in your state. There are over 17 million sole proprietorships in the US, and nearly 5 million corporations. For an elegantly simple presentation of US business statistics, visit www.bizstats.com.

SOLE PROPRIETORSHIP. A sole proprietorship often requires no special forms or fees, though you'll need a state reseller license if you are purchasing and reselling merchandise, and you may need to file a local D.B.A. (Doing Business As) if you use a made-up company name rather than your name. According to Schedule C's filed with the IRS, 1/4 of all sole proprietorships showed no profit (net income) in 2001, i.e., expenses equaled or exceeded sales. The only additional "business tax" you pay as a sole proprietor is the self employment tax. The rest of the income just ends up on your personal income tax.

GENERAL PARTNERSHIP. While verbal agreements may be legally binding, they can be pretty tough to prove if the relationship goes south. Make sure you get down on paper the assets each partner is bringing the business, a way to end or change the structure of the partnership, how profits or losses will be apportioned and paid or collected, and how decisions will be reached. Since the actions of one partner obligate the others, you better be careful, since some actions may incur unlimited liability. The taxes on a general partnership are generally charged against your personal income, though there may be an additional state form or tax schedule to fill out. Limited partnerships exist to limit liability, but you'd better have a lawyer explain what that really means. The general, or senior partner, may still have unlimited liability for expenses.

GENERAL "C" CORPORATION. A general corporation is in essence an artificial person, so the personal assets of the owners which are not brought into the corporation are generally protected. This protection of assets against liabilities is known as the "Corporate Veil." Unfortunately, since many unscrupulous businessmen men have exploited the corporate veil to their personal advantage, the courts have begun to allow certain lawsuits to pierce the veil. The cost of setting up a corporation varies from state to state, but it usually amounts to a couple hundred dollars in filing fees and a couple hundred dollars to a lawyer or accountant to do the filing. One of the great strengths of corporations is they provide a standard mechanism for raising capital from multiple investors and distributing profits, selling shares and declaring dividends. All forms of corporations involve some extra paperwork and small expenses, like purchasing a corporate seal. There may also be quarterly filings required, depending on the corporation form and the state. Regular audits by a CPA will also be required if you plan to borrow money as a corporation rather than as an individual.

"S" CORPORATION. The primary drawback of running a business as a general corporation is double taxation. Corporate profits are taxed, and excess profits that you distribute as dividends to yourself and any other shareholders are also taxed. The "S" corporation, sometimes called a family corporation, combines some of the advantages of the general corporation with the tax advantages of a sole proprietorship or general partnership. The protection an "S" corporation provides may be weaker than that of a "C" corporation, since judges are aware it is often set up for no other reason than to invoke the "corporate veil."

LIMITED LIABILITY CORPORATION (LLC). An LLC is a hybrid that combines the tax benefits of a partnership with some of the liability benefits of incorporation. This can be one of the most expensive types of business entities to set up because professional help is required both for the filing and to establish the partnership agreements. However, it's rapidly becoming more popular and is easier to set up in some states than others.

🚢 Business Practice

Organization and Job Descriptions

If you are a sole proprietor with no employees, the structure of your organization will be pretty obvious. In charge of dealing with corporate customers – YOU. In charge of cleaning the toilet – YOU. Everything else in between – YOU. But as soon as you hire anybody to do something, take on a partner, or even accept free help from family, you have an organizational challenge. The trick in a traditional business model is to create a structure where different people are responsible for different tasks, and everybody knows who is responsible for what. You don't want a technician who really isn't interested in sales quoting people ballpark prices over the phone, and you don't want a salesperson who never quite figured out the difference between Microsoft Word and Microsoft Windows suggesting a customer reformat the hard drive on the network server. Well defined job descriptions and responsibilities can also prevent a lot of petty bickering down the road when things don't get done and nobody is willing to accept the blame. In all instances, as the boss, one of your job duties is to make sure that everybody else is performing theirs.

There is another option to this business model, called "Creative Anarchy," in which everybody is responsible for everything, including delegating tasks to each other. This type of business is rarely planned, but it can actually succeed and be a great deal of fun, as long as every new hire is a bright-eyed, intelligent, eager-to-learn go-getter. In other words, it can't work out in the long run, but if you get lucky with a partner or some early hires, you can give your business a chance to find it's own way before imposing a structure and turning people into cogs. There's no reason why everybody in a small business can't become a competent technician and salesperson, though activities like purchasing and bill paying are best left in your hands. The primary danger with this happy-go-lucky approach to business is when you run out of luck hiring budding versions of yourself and end up with some average or below average employees. In the absence of tightly defined job duties and close supervision, an average Joe or Jane who would have worked out fine in a traditional business will mess-up, making both of you miserable. Unfortunately, I don't know any tricks for hiring exclusively above-average people, and part of the problem is that none may apply for the job. If you have a growing business and you need extra hands, you have to settle for the best you can find.

Scheduling and Prioritizing

Whether you're talking about a one person business or a dozen technicians and salesmen, prioritizing and scheduling tasks is a key management skill. When it comes to daily activities, sales usually takes precedence, and that's not as crazy as it first sounds. If you have a retail store and a potential customer walks in looking to buy something, are you going to say, "Wait until

I finish this build," or "Leave me alone. I'm trying to balance the books," or are you going to say, "How can I help you?" I'm not suggesting that going out and looking for new sales rather than performing warranty service is an acceptable way to run a business, though some people take that approach. However, if you pick up the phone and somebody wants to buy something, the only situation in which you should say "Let me call you back," is if you already have a customer on the other line.

Of course, sales activities themselves must also be prioritized. Don't waste your time going after business that you either won't get or can't make money on. There's no point in bidding on RFPs for which you don't meet the requirements. There's also not a whole lot of point in chasing corporate sales until you've been in business for a while and have built a list of references. You should also be cautious about pricing custom configurations and hardware you've never heard of for new accounts. It doesn't make sense to drop everything else you're doing to chase down a price on a special video capture card for some stranger on the phone who is calling everybody in the book, or to dedicate your morning to searching for a memory upgrade for an obsolete printer. The job of a salesperson is to sell the stuff you can make money on, not to cater to the whims of any potential customer on the theory that it might lead to something down the road.

Scheduling and prioritizing service calls is something of an art, and it requires a thorough knowledge of your customers, the local region, and the vendor base your business deals with. Your first consideration should always be whether or not a customer can limp by for a couple more hours with the problem they've reported, or if their business is effectively shut down. If a single workstation goes down in any kind of office, that employee can usually find something else useful to do for a few hours, but if the network server goes down, it could be costing that business thousands of dollars of lost productivity per hour. Some customers are just more aggressive than others in describing problems over the phone. I can't tell you how many times I've been given a phone message that there's an urgent problem out at some customer's, only to be met on arrival with, "You didn't need to rush over, it's really no big deal." Any time you have more than one field service call and you haven't yet talked to the best technical contact at the customer's, take the time to phone before jumping in the car.

A caveat to "sales takes precedence" is this: YOU HAVE TO FINISH THINGS. Multitasking is great for computers, but studies have shown that when people multitask, their efficiency goes to pot. All of your mental overhead goes into task swapping, and nothing gets done. For this reason, I like to schedule the easy service calls first whenever possible, just to clear items from the "to do" list. The need to complete tasks doesn't just apply to service calls, though messing up there is the surest way to alienate your customers. It applies to the whole business. If you feel that you're getting stressed, make a list of all the open issues you need to deal with, and I promise it will be too many. Take a break from looking for new business and start whittling down the list, starting with the items that are the easiest for you to close out. When you get down to a few tough nuts, you'll find them much easier to crack since your mind will no longer be distracted with a dozen other open issues.

How you schedule any PC builds or regular business overhead, such as bookkeeping, depends entirely on the scale of your business and how busy you are. If you are a one pony show and you have plenty of sales and service activity to keep you busy during regular business hours, leave the builds and the non-critical overhead functions for the evenings. The nice thing about builds is that you can start and stop working at any point, so you can whittle away at them between your other activities.

There is one critical business activity that takes priority over everything except the urgent service call, and that's billing and collecting. Never delay presenting an invoice for your products or services. If you can't do it on the spot, put it in the mail as soon as you get back to the office. Never hesitate to call up customers when bills are due, armed with your invoice number and their purchase order (P.O.) number, and ask where your money is. Nobody will be offended unless they have something to hide – IT'S YOUR MONEY.

Partners in Name and Spirit

There are two types of business partners, those who co-own a business with you and those who are employed by you but are critical to your operations. For example, if half your business is network support and you count on a single employee to do 100% of that work, you effectively have a partner. In either case, how the money is shared is less important than how the work is shared. A partnership between unequal partners doesn't stand a snowball's chance in hell. Going back to our network example, if networking was 80% of your business and either you or your "partner" is carrying that entire load, it's not going to work out in the long run. If you're the network guru, you'll eventually figure out that the other party is just overhead, and if you're the overhead, need I say more? Don't start out your business life by giving away half your business or income to a deadbeat partner in return for a headache.

Even equally participating partners must have matching goals, particularly in the financial arena. Otherwise, if success comes and one partner wants to maximize profits while the other wants to hire employees and start relaxing, you have a problem. The only way to avoid such difficulties is by regularly discussing where the business is and where it's heading. Make sure you talk in hard numbers, not in vague descriptive terms. There's no point telling your partner, "Well, if we're successful reasonably soon, we'll be able to expand next year sometime." What's your partner supposed to do aside from nod? On the other hand, if you say, "If we manage a net profit of $40,000 when we rough out the taxes in January, I think we should hire a salesmen to go after corporate accounts," your partner and you will have something to discuss. Hopefully, your partner will have the sense to tell you that it's a bad idea!

Business Relationships (Not the Romantic Kind)

"Trust" is one of the most abused words in the business vocabulary. It took Ronald Reagan to put trust in its proper place, when he invoked the Russian Proverb "Trust, but verify." The corporate purchasing manager at that new client you just landed might be a pillar of morality, and he might also be the only person in the company that doesn't know their business is teetering on the brink of bankruptcy. You'll never get anywhere suing a failed corporate entity to recover your money or goods after the fact, you'll be at the back of the line behind the banks and other primary creditors. When it comes to checking out the credit history of parties you're doing business with, you should be able to find a local library with a subscription to the Dun & Bradstreet Million Dollar Database. However, if you can't find local access or the time to get there, you can run individual reports through Hoover's online at www.hoovers.telebase.com/form.htm. The same approach goes for hiring people who actually have a work history. If they give references, check them. If all of their old employers are out of business or won't verify anything other than their dates of employment, I'd take a pass. Likewise when a new vendor tells you it will be there first thing in the morning, don't bet your most valuable customer on it. People lie. People are ignorant. Trust but verify.

On the positive side, good business relationships are one of things that make being in business worthwhile. If you're good at what you do, don't overcharge, and launder your clothes on a regular basis, your customers will come to like you and recommend you to their friends. Good relationships with your professional colleagues will provide you with somebody to talk to (free therapy, providing you pay for the meal), and a resource to fall back on when you have trouble solving a problem. Your peers are your best source for business advice of all kinds. It takes somebody who has run a business on a shoestring to relate to your problems and offer practical solutions. People without small business experience think that financing is all about shopping for a good interest rate.

Volunteers and Other Losing Propositions

If your mother or your son wants to volunteer in your business, great. Whatever problems arise, you're a family, so they would have crept up sooner or later anyway. The type of volunteering I'm talking about amounts to working on spec (speculation that something paying will arise). This can be as seemingly harmless as the neighborhood kid who will do anything to learn how PCs are put together to the out-of-work professional trying to retrain in a new field. Volunteers in business are dangerous and should not be accepted. I've never known a volunteering scenario to end on a happy note. I've seen many examples of "mutually beneficial" relationships that were clearly defined at the onset dissolve into recriminations, "confiscated" equipment, even lawsuits. If the neighborhood kid wants it so bad, work something out with the parents and pay in second-hand hardware, but don't accept free help.

Adult volunteers are much more dangerous than kids, because they always have ulterior motives. They generally use volunteering as a way to worm into a business that wouldn't gamble on hiring them otherwise, or to front their own private activities. You never want somebody who doesn't work for you being associated with your business. When an angry IT manager comes storming into your office and threatening to sue you over the destruction of their network, your insistence that "that guy doesn't actually work for me – I just let him use a desk and a phone" isn't going to cut it. Many volunteers are living on insurance claims or working some other scam that doesn't allow them to show an income, so I wouldn't bet heavily on their innate honesty. If you tango with a skunk you can expect to get sprayed. Face it. If some one has nothing better to do than to hang around your business for free, there's probably a reason for that.

Outside salespeople, as opposed to inside salespeople who answer the phone and take orders, usually expect commission to play a large part in their overall compensation. Some inside salespeople also earn commission, but it's usually a lower proportion of their income. You better make sure to structure your commission deal so your salespeople can't get rich by selling your products at a loss. Although the math gets a little complicated, it's probably best to pay commission on gross profit, without trying to take all of your fixed costs into account. The actual commission percentage will be dependent on the base pay of the salesperson, with a high base pay receiving a low commission.

One way of establishing a commission percentage is to decide on a yearly salary figure you'd be happy paying out for a certain level of sales volume. Then subtract the base pay of the salesperson from that number, leaving you with the total amount of commission the salesperson would need to earn to reach that level. Divide the total amount of commission by the net profit you calculate for that sales volume using your standard margin, and you get the commission percentage. Note that your standard margin can only be arrived at through experience, though we gave a few rules of thumb earlier. The reason for paying commission based on the cost of goods, money and delivery is to give the salesperson a reason to do business with customers that pay on time, aren't located in Gnome, and aren't beating you to death on your standard margin.

For example, say you estimate a decent income for a salesperson is $60K a year (don't kid yourself, a real salesperson isn't going to work for free), but you keep the base salary down to $30K. That leaves $30K the salesperson must earn in commission to get to the $60K salary. Now say you expect that salesperson to do $1,000,000 in volume for the year. At your standard margin of 20 points for working out of commercial space, $1,000,000 in gross sales gives you $200,000 in gross profit. Divide the $30,000 of commission you think is fair by the $200,000, and you get 15%. We used these numbers to keep the math simple, but 20 points is certainly too low for the basic margin when your operation is employing a full time salesperson. Ideally, you should back the whole $60K of salesperson compensation out of your margin, meaning you need to make $1,000,000 gross profit on $740,000 in sales, or a 26 point margin. Don't forget that the cost of the salesperson doesn't end with the salary and commission. The employer social security contribution you need to make, not to mention other benefits and footing the bill for necessary sales expenses means that the salesperson who earns $60K in compensation will run you at least $80K in actual outlay. Of course, all of these numbers are really based on a hardware focused business. A salesperson selling high margin training or software support will expect a higher commission.

You'll also notice that if the salesperson sells $2,000,000 worth of stuff, they pick up an additional $30K in commission and $90K on the year, but if they only manage $500,000 in sales, their take is down to $15K and $45K on the year. This brings up the very real question of whether it makes sense for you to spend $45K a year (plus benefits and social security) to do an additional $500,000 in sales, and the answer is most likely "no." One way to adjust for this is to pay a lower commission for sales up to some figure, and a higher commission after that, such as 10% for the first million in sales, 20% afterwards. But you can see where hand-waving like this is likely to lead. You can try for a lower base pay to attract hungrier salespeople, but they won't have much experience. If you can possibly run your operation without full time sales positions, as most small computer business do, you'll be much better off. As we stated earlier, if you can't sell yourself, you should think twice about going into business for yourself.

Want a Peanut?
Care and Feeding of the Elephant Customer

The majority of bad feelings in business arise from broken promises. Promises about delivery dates, promises about reliability, promises about support, and promises about whatever it is the product or service can do to benefit the customer. You should never promise customers more than you can deliver, but when does it make sense to deliver more than you promised? It's not at all uncommon for a small computer business to derive more than half their income from a single customer, who I call the "Elephant Customer." I even know of cases of entrepreneurs who were put into business by an elephant customer, often a former employer who wanted to concentrate on their core business. However you land a pachyderm, it's clear that a different set of rules apply. While you still need to make money on the elephant, you clearly can't afford to lose it either. The best way to keep your elephant happy is to deliver even more than you promise, primarily in the area of time.

Whenever I've had a lot of ongoing business with a single customer, I've made it a practice to drop in on a regular basis just to make sure everything is running OK. I also handle the quickie hardware and software troubleshooting jobs without charging, even on stuff that I didn't sell them. I make a real effort to educate the primary decision maker on how to save money, even if it means slightly lower sales for me, and I teach them as much as they're willing to learn about their computer systems. I recently completed a five year long project with an elephant, in which I didn't charge for about 20% of the hours I was on site, and I don't regret a single one of them. I also charged a much lower rate than the norm for the work I was doing, but the length of the relationship more than made up for it. No matter how good you are at what you do, you're going to have some unhappy customers. In the business jungle, keep your elephant happy and if a rhesus monkey hangs out in the tree throwing rotten fruit at you, shrug it off.

Firing Customers

The customer is not always right. Some customers are so nearly always wrong it will be necessary to fire them. Aside from the fact there's nothing to be gained from stretching out the experience until both parties are permanently unhappy, it can cost you a lot of money. I don't know the legal implications of telling somebody flat out that you don't want to do any more business with them, but there are many more subtle ways to get the point across. Pricing yourself out of the market, for example, or insisting on written contracts at the customer's expense. Implementing a sudden change of "business focus" is another possibility, as in "We are re-assessing whether we can do that sort of work in the future." Warranty work must be carried out to term, but you can get pretty strict as to what exactly is and isn't your responsibility.

Years ago, a company I was working for made a special deal for a new customer who was going to bring us a couple thousand dollars a week in business. Meeting his price required us to buy hardware outside our regular channels and to reduce our margin to the risky point, but his business sounded so attractive that we couldn't let him walk out without a deal. Well, I don't know if he simply based his proposition on overly optimistic projections or if he was lying through his teeth, but the volume he promised never materialized. And we were treating him like an elephant, well, for peanuts. I finally got rid of him when he came strolling in with a $10 keyboard for a warranty exchange. After checking the paperwork, I told him he was out of luck. The keyboard was one day beyond its warranty period. Never saw him again. He didn't like being treated like rhesus monkey. A young woman I was training as a technician at the time was shocked, as she had this image of me always being a "nice guy." I am a nice guy, but not to people who take advantage of me.

I'm Going to Sue You (Or Tell My Mommy)

When things do go wrong in business, the first words out of somebody's mouth are likely to be "I'm going to sue you!" In my opinion, this is the post-kindergarten equivalent of "I'm going to tell my mommy on you." It's something people say when they run out of everything else, and unfortunately, some people do act on it. I've never been sued, so my experience here is strictly second-hand, but I can say that the first thing you have to do is go out and get a lawyer of your own. The second thing is to get all of your documentation together so that you aren't making extra trips to the lawyer (at several hundred dollars an hour). Documentation can consist not only of receipts, invoices, quotes and written agreements, but also any notes you have about work in progress, phone conversations, etc. This is where files come in handy, one per customer, where you include every scrap of paper having to do with that customer. Lawyers live for paper, so don't be sparing.

If there is any chance at all to avoid going to court, I'd take it. It's not just your time, it's all the money you'll be paying lawyers. If the issues at the heart of the problem are just so emotionally charged that you can't discuss the problem like mature adults, consider arbitration. There are professional arbitrators who will settle non-criminal disputes for a fee, which is likely to be cheaper than court costs. Most of the lawsuits I've seen have come about after one party has gone out of business and there's really not much chance of the injured party accomplishing much aside from putting the lawyer's kid through Harvard. The exception is probably nickel-dime insurance claims. I once wrote a deposition for a customer who had been sold a false bill of goods by a computer store that later went out of business. They received damages from the insurance company to allow them to purchase a new server to replace the hunk of obsolete garbage they'd been sold, but that only amounted to a few thousand dollars, or less than the typical auto accident claim.

Remaining Sane

Small businesses have a way of taking over your life. If you're a workaholic, it's even more dangerous to be in business for yourself than to be working for other people, because an employer may have the sense to lock you out of the office one day a week. The best system I know for retaining some small measure of sanity was invented thousands of years ago, and can be summed up as "Remember the Sabbath Day and Keep it Holy." I don't care which Sabbath day you propose to take off, though if your business is in the US there's some advantage to making it Sunday, and I don't care whether you go out somewhere to worship God or if you stay home and worship television. The key is not to answer your business phone, not to go into the office (especially a home office) and most important of all, not to go near a computer.

Nobody I know would call me a religious Jew, but my computer remains off from dusk on Friday evening until I see three stars out on Saturday night, and I credit this practice with keeping me partially sane. The funny thing is I actually go a little nuts on Saturdays trying to fill the time, but knowing that I'm not going to send or respond to any e-mail keeps me from obsessing about ongoing work. I was working with one other guy some years ago, and we had a 24x7 support contract with a customer who wasn't shy about calling. I was planning on taking off my first two days in eight months of work for Rosh HaShanna, the Jewish New Year. Since I was going to synagogue both days, I told the other guy I'd be home in the after-

ALPHA MOM

noons, but not to call me unless it was a real emergency. I got called in both days. Better to be a little religious and let your customers and co-workers know. People respect that, and you'll get some rest.

🚢 BUSINESS PSYCHOLOGY

Setting Goals and Knowing When to Quit

The owner of the first computer start-up I ever worked for, after expanding from four employees to thirty-five full time workers in less than a year, was asked, "How much is enough?" His answer was, "I don't know." The business sank with all hands onboard less than six months later. If you don't have a goal, you can't ever win. If you want to target replacing Dell as the largest mail-order PC maker in the world, that's just fine, but if you should happen to manage it, step back and think about what you're doing before you take on Microsoft and IBM. Computer entrepreneurs are especially vulnerable to the lure of low hanging fruit – seemingly profitable businesses that your customers are just begging you to enter into. Some people consider goal setting the heart and soul of a good business plan, but I think it has more to do with the individual's psychology. Just like there are compulsive gamblers who need to bet until they lose it all, there are compulsive expanders, who need to grow their business beyond their ability to manage it successfully.

About the most reasonable explanation for neurosis that psychologists can offer is that it arises from irreconcilable inner conflicts. In other words, neurotic people are constantly at war with themselves, or at least with their idealized self-image. The easiest way to guarantee eventual failure in business is to set conflicting goals for yourself. Since the individual goals may be quite reasonable taken by themselves, this can easily happen. If you set yourself the goal of earning over $250,000 a year in profits without taking on employees, that's very admirable. If you set yourself the goal of being the best little PC repair shop in the neighborhood, that's also very admirable. The only problem is you can't make over $250K a year repairing neighborhood PCs in a one technician shop. Best forget about the repair shop and become a corporate trainer or software consultant, or forget about the $250K. Otherwise, you're going to end up running a business that needs a therapist, and who's going to pay for that?

There are two good reasons to quit the PC business. First, you've accomplished everything you wanted, and now you want to sell the business and move on to the next challenge. Second, it's not working out. It turns out that with the exception of public figures, like basketball and movie stars, people have a much easier time walking away from success than failure. That may be because we Americans are brought up to believe that giving up is the primary reason for failure. While persistence may pay off in courtship, it can cost you everything you own in business. On second thought, it can do that in courtship too, but at least your assets will go to somebody you once loved, rather than creditors. If you have a working spouse or some other source of income that pays the bills, you can fool around at break-even for a couple years and hope that you learn the trick of turning a profit. However, if you are the sole source of support for yourself and your family, you better learn quickly how to differentiate between optimism and stupidity.

Flexibility and Changing with the Times

When you first start out in business, you might be justified in believing that any customer is a good customer, especially if you need immediate income to get by. Unfortunately, lots of small transactions are a really tough way to make a living, even if you have a retail shop and walk in traffic. As both you and your business grow, you should evaluate what kind of customers you really want to pursue. If you are proud of being stubborn, there's a good chance you'll get in trouble, because the business will always be changing. For example, if you have a successful retail operation and then a chain store opens up at the mall, odds are your current business model will no longer work. Success never goes unnoticed, and generally results in competition. You can only expand so far training regular folks how to use PCs before you start losing business to new competition willing to work for half your price. Maybe you've established a great reputation building websites for small businesses, but what do you do once you've sold one to everybody in town?

The key to surviving in business long term is to never stop learning. This doesn't mean accumulating certifications by cramming for multiple choice tests. Nor does it mean putting all of your spare time into playing with some new operating system or application that you believe will become the next Windows or Office. Your customers are the only people who can tell you what direction they are moving in, and learning new skills to support your current customers needs makes a lot more sense than trying to find new customers for some product or service that strikes your fancy. Customers who don't employ their own full time computer person will even pay you as you learn, which is a double win. It's also much easier to move into a new area if you have real experience and references, as opposed to having fooled around with it at home.

Watch out that you don't become to complacent about your expertise. Recently, to avoid becoming a third wheel on a shopping trip, I told a friend to "just buy the laser printer that fits your price range, they're all compatible with Windows." My friend came back with the new HP LaserJet 1000 for around $250. I love HP printers. I had an original LaserJet over fifteen years ago, and I bought a model 1200 just last summer. However, as I looked over the instructions (surprise) prior to hooking it up for him, I noticed that the operating system compatibility started with Windows 98. My friend's notebook, a hand-me-down from his brother, had Windows 95 installed. The printer turned out to be USB only (no printer port support), which is one of the reasons they dropped compatibility for operating system versions where the bugs hadn't been ironed out of USB yet. The HP website made it clear that it wasn't supported by any version of Windows 95, and the notebook didn't support USB in any case, so I had my friend return it and get a Brother, which even had drivers for Windows 3.1 and DOS.

The moral of the story is that the industry does make changes from time to time, and you can get in deep water by being too complacent. It had never occurred to me that anybody would manufacture laser printers without printer ports! In this case, it was an easily returned printer for a friend (fortunately, I never broke open the toner cartridge which could result in a restocking fee). It could just have easily been a number of mail-order printers for a job that would have been difficult and expensive to return, and left me looking pretty stupid with a customer.

A Man For All Seasons

Hiring and Firing

I've interviewed and hired people for full-time work only as an employee for others. I mention this just to push the point that if you can avoid having employees, especially while you're still learning the business, you'll save yourself a ton of grief. Regular employees require workers compensation insurance (workers comp), matching social security payments, payroll tax deductions and the associated accounting, and unemployment tax contributions. Employees also make it more complicated (i.e. expensive) for you to implement a Self Employed Pension Plan (SEP) which can save you thousands of dollars a year on your taxes. Throughout this book I've emphasized that if you can avoid taking on employees, you'll save yourself a big headache. Even if you stick to hiring independent contractors, you may be liable to special reporting requirements. For example, in Massachusetts, my home turf, all employers, regardless of size or type of business, are required to report new hires to the Massachusetts Department of Revenue within 14 days of hire. They use this information to catch people who aren't paying their child support, and you may be required to garnish wages for the DOR, even for an independent contractor.

If you are successful in business, you may find yourself forced to choose between expanding and turning down perfectly good business. If you resist expansion, you may even start losing customers who want one-stop shopping for all of their needs. So, if you've gone as far as you can using contract (1099) help and strategic relationships with other businesses, you might just have to bite the bullet and start hiring. The first step is to get an EIN (Employer Identification Number) by filing Form SS-4 with the IRS. This nine-digit number is for use on tax forms specifically where it's asked for by name, it's not a substitute for your social security number. You can get an EIN immediately by applying over the phone to Tele-TIN (1-866-816-2065 at last notice).

If you do have to hire employees, start with part-timers. You can do worse than sticking with a combination of working moms for the mornings and students in the afternoons. I've had reasonable luck hiring co-op students from universities, something I support in part because I was a co-op myself, but there are so few engineering students these days that you may be unable to attract any or have to pay too much. On the other hand, you may find business students, or even political science majors, who are decent computer techs from having grown up with it as a hobby, and who have impressive inter-personal and sales skills.

At first blush it might seem that the only route to go is part-timers. After all, you'll save on unemployment insurance and any other benefits, they're much easier to fire and you can sample a larger number of prospective employees. An often overlooked advantage with part-timers is that you can schedule several of them to work at the same time, turning your business into a four or five person concern at peak retail hours or during big installs. However, part-timers also have their drawbacks, primarily that it's just not a career for them. A full time employee is far less likely to quit in order to go on Spring Break or to take a fling at some other interest. Also, the overhead of constantly training and managing new part-timers can eat seriously into the time you hoped to save by hiring them. Finally, customers like a sense of stability, particularly when dealing with small businesses, and they don't want to have a different person show up every time they call for service.

When hiring technicians, the main thing I look for is initiative. In other words, if I'm interviewing somebody and I have to ask all the questions, I'm not going to hire that person. I don't worry much about experience unless I'm looking for a senior person, and I don't give a hoot for certifications because I've never had a field service call where the customer needed help filling out a multiple choice test! I want somebody who can tell a story about some problem they solved, whether it's computer related or not. I also believe in paying above average wages, but it only makes sense if you're careful about finding above average people. The best chance for an employer/ employee relationship to work out is when both parties get what they want. Don't hire somebody who wants full time work for a part-time job, and don't promise on-the-job training to an aspiring technician who you really want as a receptionist. Make sure you get a feel for whether or not a management candidate wants responsibility. One time when I was trying to help straighten out a foundering computer company, their tech manager plainly said, "I just want somebody to tell me what to do." The guy was a fine technician, but he was in over his head as a manager, and he was clearly telling anybody who would listen. Unfortunately, and not surprisingly, the management problems in the company didn't end with him.

If there is one exercise you can go through that might save your business down the road, it's to look into the eyes of each person you are thinking of hiring and ask yourself, "Could I fire this person if things get tight?" If the answer is no, don't make the hire. For starters, make it clear to new employees that they are being hired on a trial basis, so they shouldn't sell their house and buy one next door to you. Although it may sound funny at first, one of the most important things you can do when it comes to protecting yourself from your own employees is to prepare and distribute a company handbook that includes a written termination policy. Termination policies usually include immediate dismissal for criminal behavior such as theft, violence, harassment, etc.. Give employees clear warnings if they aren't living up to your expectations. Be specific, as in, "I won't be able to send you out on service calls if you make that mistake again," or "If I have to tell you again that I want it done this way, I'm going to have to let you go." Some businesses even give multiple written warnings. Have a bulletproof explanation prepared and don't allow the occasion to become a bargaining session. When you decide somebody must go, send them home with the stuff in their desk (if they had one), and pay them whatever is coming to them. This is one of those occasions where you might want to pay for a bit of lawyer time up front just to get it right, because there are lots of lawsuits in this area, and even if you win, you lose time and legal costs. The person you let go may feel they have nothing to lose by suing you, and their legal costs might even be paid for by the State or Federal government if they accuse you of discrimination or a labor law violation.

🚢 GREY AREAS

I vs. We

One of the simplest and cheapest ways you can improve your business image is to get into the habit of referring to yourself as "We." The truth is, I was never able to manage it myself, but I've seen it in action with almost all of the successful sole proprietors I know. When some of these consultants say we, they mean, "Me and the guy at Mailboxes etc," or "Me and my kids, if they'll just answer the phone after school," but it goes a long way in projecting the image of a "company" rather than some guy off the street. Your friends and family might make fun of you when "we" becomes so ingrained that you start using it for "I" all the time, but if it worked for the old English royalty, it can work for you.

On the other hand, I wouldn't snow customers as to the boundaries between your business and other businesses. If you have a reseller agreement with say, IBM, it's normal to refer to "IBM and I" as "We" when pitching a sale, but it's criminal misrepresentation to pass yourself off as an IBM employee. It's also a good idea to have a clear idea of just who "We" is, so if somebody asks you about your company, you won't choke on your tongue. If "We" means "Me and Moe who's doing the hardware support," that's probably all the customer will want to know. If they ask if Moe is an employee, as long as Moe has agreed to do the work, you can say that you have a contractual relationship. I've never actually seen these questions come up, most people just accept the "We" at face value.

Compulsive Confession

On the opposite end of the spectrum from "We'ing" is the art of compulsive confession. This is generally practiced by soon-to-be ex-businessmen, who are so paranoid about taking on any responsibility or leaving themselves open to criticism, that they tell the customer far more than the customer wants to know. In fact, they tell the customer so much about their own short-comings and what could go wrong in the worst case scenario that they effectively un-sell themselves. The customer doesn't need to hear about your problems with your current supplier, the fact that you accidentally bounced a check last week, or that you only passed "C+" programming in college with a "D+." If you're only willing to do a job on the basis that the customer accepts all responsibility and pays you an hourly rate, what you're really saying is that you want to be an employee.

Compulsive confession may take a load off your chest, but it puts it all on the customer, which is hardly what they are hiring you for. Don't confuse it with honesty. You're rarely going to get the opportunity to make people a 100% guarantee in life, but that doesn't mean you need to 100% persuade them that something might go wrong. If a person asks me whether their credit card information is safe on the Internet, I always say "Yes." Sure, there are things that can go wrong, but the weakest link is probably a dishonest employee at the outfit that they are purchasing from, not some whiz-bang hacker. When you give your credit card to a waiter at a restaurant, do you worry if the transaction is secure? When you fix a computer and the customer asks, "Is it fixed?" the answer is "Yes." That's what "fixed" means. If you start explaining that 1 out of 1000 new hard drives fails in the first week of operation, according to the bathtub curve of probability, you aren't doing them any favors, you're just giving them something to worry about.

Software Piracy and OEM structures

When it comes to software piracy, I draw the line at selling people pirated software, a practice I've never consciously engaged in. Why the "consciously" qualifier? Well, when Microsoft first introduced OEM software manufacturing, there was a lot of piracy in the open market, sometimes called the "grey" market. Certain companies were advertising and selling OEM operating systems that they had been granted a license to produce and sell with hardware, but they far exceeded the number of copies they were allowed to manufacture. Since everybody in the clone business depends on OEM operating systems for new PCs, and since the actual product was identical, it was very easy to get taken in by a pirate. In the end, the easiest way to differentiate between legal and illegal software is price. If one outfit is selling Microsoft software for less than everybody else, be it 20% or 50%, it may be pirated. The holograms and serial numbers haven't seemed to impact the pirate's ability to turn out perfect copies. There is a hotline for software piracy where you can check up on suppliers or rat people out at 1-888-NO-PIRACY or log on at www.bsa.org. The whole point of Microsoft discounting OEM software, by the way, is that the OEM undertakes support of the product.

The other thing about software that almost everybody ignores is that it's licensed rather than sold. It is licensed to the individual who purchases it new, and the license is often not transferable. This is completely ignored in the second-hand market, by buyers, sellers, and even the software manufacturers. However, I always point it out to people who contact me from charities looking for large numbers of donated computers. If you're going to be involved in transferring hundreds or thousands of PCs from one party to another, like from a big company to a girl's school in Afghanistan, you better check with the software manufacturers whose software is installed on those machines, including the operating system. I would be truly surprised if they didn't come across with a waiver to allow the transfer to occur legally or supply you with some new-old software that they can write-off. Besides, big companies are extremely careful about what happens to their old PCs these days for fear of being sued over improper disposal of hazardous waste or violation of software licensing agreements. I've even heard of big insurance companies paying $50 per serial number just to get the PCs off their books. Therefore, if you want to approach a big business looking for free PCs for charity, you better get the legal issues straight first.

Deposits for Custom Work and Restocking Fees

When it comes to custom work in any business, the standard practice is to require a non-refundable deposit to cover your risk, typically around 20% for custom PCs. Many electronics businesses charge "restocking" fees on the order of 15% for items sold in retail boxes that are returned, sometimes dependent on whether or not the box was opened. Auto parts stores often refuse to accept returns of any electronic components, in

MTBF (Mean Time Between Failures)

part to discourage swap-till-you-drop "troubleshooting" at their expense. Now, just because everybody has these policies posted in large lettering behind the counter, doesn't mean it's legal. The laws governing this area of commerce are usually legislated on the state level, so you need to do some investigating on your own or talk to a lawyer if you want to be sure that the law is on your side. I suspect that these policies are often posted without regard to their legality, to impress upon customers that irresponsible purchasing really hurts the business they patronize. Many states have "buyer's remorse" laws that allow customers to return anything within X days for no reason. Be aware that there are also some sick individuals who live for credit card disputes, constantly refusing to pay their bills for trumped up reasons, and leaving it to the credit card company and the vendor to work it out between them.

Custom software work may not require any out-of-pocket expenses on your part, but your time is money and the hours can mount up quickly. If you are working as a completely independent contractor on a pay-for-performance project, rather than an hourly rate, it's crucial to establish milestones at which partial payments will be made. Milestones are verifiable stages of progress in the coding that can be demonstrated to work, and documentation for that part of the project should be completed at the same time. In my personal experience, the greatest stumbling block to customer satisfaction on software projects is joint failure to accurately define the job before beginning. My earliest lesson in this was on a co-op job for a military contractor 16 years ago. After a single "what do you want" session, with no software design set down on paper, I wrote them a custom database in BASIC (their choice) that met all their stated requirements. The problem was, they hadn't really thought it through that well, and I failed to ask them enough questions or to demonstrate any intermediate stages. The 'minor" changes they wanted in the finished program meant I had to rewrite it from scratch, and you know what? The same thing happened when I completed the next version. Since this job of writing the database was secondary to my other work there, I procrastinated finishing the third version until right before the summer was over and I was headed back to school. Frankly, I don't know if they ever used it or not, but the point is, you can't write software for somebody else based on assumptions and expect them to be happy. The hardest part of programming is often just getting the basic functional design of what the customer wants down on paper and agreed to, with a set of milestones for payment.

Warranty Parts Exchange

Just about everybody offers a one year warranty on parts and service, and any new parts you buy will have a minimum of a one year manufacturer's warranty. The trick is whether you do onsite service or depot service only. For those of you working out of your houses, it probably makes more sense to do onsite service as a habit, and that may be necessary to compete with the Dells and Gateways in any case. Because the turn-around time for failed parts on RMA (Return Merchandise Authorization) can often be measured in weeks or months rather than days, you may have to cover the repair out of pocket. Keeping anybody's machine in your shop for a minute longer than you have to is bad for customer relations and leads to clutter, liability exposure and time management problems. Warranty repair turnaround is normally guaranteed for one business day. In cases like a rare motherboard or top of the line CPU where you can't afford or just don't want to own a duplicate, you should be prepared to offer a "loaner" – a somewhat equivalent machine. This is one of the reasons I encourage the use of a small number of suppliers with whom you build good relationships, because they will cross-ship warranty exchange parts for you. It's also why you should favor suppliers who can ship to you by UPS ground and have the part show up within 24 hours.

The saving grace is that to the best of my flawed understanding, it's legal to do warranty repair with used parts, providing you include the option in your written warranty. Check with your State's Attorney General office. Many major manufacturer warranties refer to repair with "remanufactured" parts in the small print. This means that at first you'll have to buy parts as problems arise, such as video cards, modems, memory. When the failed part you RMA (Return Merchandise Authorization, used as a verb) comes back, it becomes your repair stock. This does not grant an open license to stock up on parts. If you go out and buy one of everything, you'll still own most of it when it's not good for anything. I've been known to cannibalize my office machines for repair parts, restoring the ripped system when the exchange part came through, but it's not a good practice. I've seen cannibalizing go terribly wrong with undisciplined tech managers who sacrifice builds in progress to get noisy customers off their backs, resulting in a downward spiral of scavenged systems. The leading indicator of cannibalism in a PC shop is case shells that have been robbed of their power supply. The practice is common because a cheap case and power supply cost less than a quality boxed power supply by itself. If you must indulge in this practice, at least throw the empty shells in the recycling bin, because you're never going to use them and they make a depressing mess.

There is no secret trick to dealing with the warranty repair issues, especially if you sell custom systems rather than cookie-cutter jobs. If you run a busy business, simply obtaining the RMA and getting the failed parts boxed up and shipped out can seem like an insurmountable task. In most PC shops you can find a variety of the less expensive parts: floppy and CD drives, cheaper adapters and mice that could have been exchanged on RMA, but have been left to rust as a loss. Also, some vendors (primarily importers) play musical chairs with RMAs, sending your bad parts to somebody else and visa-versa, on the theory you probably misdiagnosed the problem to start with. It's way too easy to convince yourself that it's not worth your time and $5 for shipping to exchange a floppy drive for another that might not work anyway, when a new one only costs $10. I used to try to group my RMAs to save on shipping, which worked fine when I ran everything, but when you get other people involved, parts start falling between the cracks. I've seen thousands, if not tens of thousands of dollars in RMA spoilage in loosely run PC companies.

Warranty Pass Through

Pretty much all PCs are sold with a one-year warranty for parts and labor, often on-site. Premiums to this warranty can include extending it out to three years (the useful life of most PCs) or guaranteeing same day, on site service. There used to be quite a few OEMs who gave five year warrantees, but I don't think any of them actually remained in business that long (surprise!). The only time I ever even look at giving longer warranties is when required by bid specs, and then use a third-party warranty provider to meet the bid. A quick aside on the subject. I used to get a lot of calls from national warranty providers who were looking for a service person in the local area. The general deal is that they overnight a suspect part in to you, you go out to the customer's and replace it, then you invoice the warranty provider a set fee, like $90. Well, the first couple of parts of the process worked fine, but payment was a slow or never proposition. Could be they've gotten better, but I wouldn't do more than one or two service calls for any national warranty outfit before getting paid.

It turns out that many of the parts you use to build a PC, particularly if they were specified by the customer and shipped to you in retail packs, have warranties longer than a year. This ranges from three to five years on hard drives, to lifetime on some modems and video cards. Some brand-name memory carries a lifetime warranty, and some monitors have tube warranties exceeding the rest of the unit. I don't advocate passing through longer warranties. For one thing, it puts too much load on you to keep the required paperwork around indefinitely to do exchanges. Besides, warranty exchanges take time, and you can't hand out a new modem to every customer with a two year old failed modem while waiting for a repaired unit that you can't sell as new to come back from the manufacturer. The problem with simply passing all the paperwork on to the customer and telling them that they have extended parts warranties if they contact the component manufacturer directly is that you are likely to be dragged into the process. While you remain responsible for parts and labor under one year, are you responsible for labor after a year if they get a free exchange part? Not unless you're foolish enough to offer.

Office Politics

Petty disputes over things like whose turn it is to make the coffee or where to set the thermostat can lead to an environment in which little or no cooperative work gets done. That's office politics in a nutshell. People are political animals, which can lead to a situation where employees spend all their time forming factions and plotting to overthrow the king. The only way to avoid a breakout of office politics in your own business is to troubleshoot each situation that arises the same way you'd approach a field service job. Establish what is working in the office before trying to figure out what's gone wrong. Otherwise, you're likely to get caught up in the latest grievance that has only the most tenuous relation to the core problem. In the most extreme case, if your employees can't get along with one another like mature adults, it's time to make some personnel changes.

The more complicated side of office politics is dealing with infighting at your client's workplace. Here you have no authority or mandate to sort things out, but you may be stuck spending appreciable time listening to both sides, particularly if you are doing long term software development or training on site. It isn't always possible to get people to stop pouring all the office dirt in your ears without offending them. Unfortunately, simply listening to people's complaints invariably results in the assumption that you are on their side. If they catch you later giving the "enemy" a sympathetic ear, they feel betrayed. If you try to act as peacemaker, you just get it from both sides, as peacemakers always do. The worst part is that the office politics are often so much more interesting than the work that it's really tough not to get involved. The closest thing to a solution I've ever come up with is to make it clear to the "revolutionaries" that wherever your sympathies lie, your responsibility is to do the best for the management who brought you in and pays your bills. Hopefully, that will make them worry you're a spy and they'll leave you alone.

⚓ TRUISMS REVISITED

Keep Expenses Down

Plan your business to fit your financing and skills. Don't spend all of your savings and mortgage your house in order to start on a grand scale. If you can't make it on a small scale first, committing tens of thousands of dollars to a fancy storefront or the best equipped training center in town isn't likely to help. The infrastructure required to run a computer business is truly minimal. All of the industrial racking, test benches and office furniture you might see in an established competitor is a convenience, not a necessity.

Managing money is not "one of the things" you need to do to be successful in business; it's THE thing. If you are accustomed to running your life with credit card debt, you better find a partner or a spouse who is willing to handle the business side of your business and treat you as an employee. The main expense you face when going into business is replacing the salary you're losing by not working for somebody else. This is a far tougher nut than any start-up expenses, and it goes on forever. The temptation to "spend money to make money" is as strong for grizzled business veterans as it is for rookies, but you have to be sure that the money you're spending will generate returns. When business is slow, it's common to throw money at advertising without really analyzing why business is slow. When business is strong, it's easy to lay out money on new pipe dreams of getting rich quick. Just because you start making money with your right hand is no reason you should start blowing it with your left. Ignore wide-eyed friends and salesmen who encourage you to "roll the dice, it's all or nothing." Building a business is not all or nothing, it's a slow process that takes most people years to get where they're comfortable with what they've built.

One of the most risky paths into business is to get help from people who make their living from helping you start a business. There are honest and successful franchisers in the world, but there are probably more individuals who make their whole income by selling the franchises as opposed to sharing in the profits from successful new locations. Any franchise that can't guarantee you customers isn't even worth looking at. Business consultants who promise to help you "put systems in place, establish good practices and enhance profits" are often nothing but parasites. You're a smart person, so read a couple more books, and learn how to do these things yourself. Once you get started, you're going to find out that you know more about your business than anybody else, and if you need specific advice, stick with accounting or legal professionals who charge by the hour.

My favorite tax deduction is retirement savings. You get to lower your personal income tax, and the money remains yours. The only other good deductions are those that increase your income through productivity gains, like an electric screwdriver, or that are plain necessary to conduct your business, like rent or insurance. It's important to run a tax efficient business, so you should really make an effort to become familiar with the tax forms, even if you're going to pay somebody else to do the filing for you. Add-ons to small business software, such as Quickbooks, can provide one-stop shopping for pretty much all of your financial needs, including credit card processing, payroll and taxes.

You can be too trusting in business and you can easily get burned so bad that you'll never recover. When your business or your personal credit is on the line for a big deal, don't be shy about hiring a lawyer and having a contract drawn up. Check out the finances of the other party, and don't be afraid to ask embarrassing questions, like, "Is it true you've filed for Chapter 11?" The same caution goes for employees. Always request references and always check them. There are lots of serial business killers out there, who ruin one small business after another with their high salaries and negative contribution. One warning sign of a deadly employee is somebody who acts in the interview like they're doing you a favor by even considering employment.

Be Tough and Fair

Most business deals are negotiated. When you first start out, you're going to have to shop around the prices people quote you for goods and services because frankly, you have no way of knowing what they're really worth. Once you do know what things are worth, at least to you, you're in the position to start negotiating. That doesn't mean that vendors will sell you things at the price you want to pay, but you certainly don't have to pay the price they want to charge. The hardest part of being tough is remembering to be fair. You aren't going to become successful by getting either your vendors or your customers to hate you. Try to find the middle ground where the deal is fair for both parties. Whether you're naturally aggressive or you learn it through practice, you have to be careful not to push people around. You can profit in the short run by being tough as nails, but in the long run, it's being fair that will get you where you want to go.

If selling PCs is a big part of your business, you need to quickly settle on a limited number of vendors and build relationships with them. Unless you're building high performance custom systems, you'll save a lot of headaches if you buy pre-built bare-bones systems that you can finish up at your shop. When you do a lot of business with one or two vendors, defective parts returns and technical support becomes much smoother and the time you save will more than make up for minor price differences. You still need to shop around occasionally to keep your prime vendors honest, but it's as much in their interest to have steady customers as it is in yours to have reliable suppliers. Mid-tier vendors aren't going to rush to extend you credit, but if you do enough business with them, it will accelerate the process.

Selling cheap PCs is a problem for a number of reasons, but primarily because you won't earn enough money per unit to justify the support and warranty service you'll be expected to provide. Whether you build inexpensive PCs yourself or buy them through the channel, they end up being less reliable and shorter lived than PCs built with higher quality components. Quality doesn't mean the best or most expensive, but the cheapest stuff is unlikely to be even mediocre. If some customer walks in out of the blue and wants discount pricing for multiple machines, don't do it unless all the machines are being ordered at once.

Unless you have a retail location, you have no excuse to buy anything in quantity for stock except the lowest priced components, such as keyboards or modems. Inventory is like a live piggy bank with a slow digestive track. Would you feed a pig hundred dollar bills for safekeeping? Computer components all lose value with time and even the parts that seem safe, such as cases, become obsolete when power supply standards change. For the same reason, you should never procrastinate returning failed hardware. Every day it sits in your shop it loses value, and you're less likely to be able to find the paperwork to get an RMA, even if it's still under warranty.

Manage Your Customers

It's tough to go wrong in the service business following the old formula *Primum non nocere*: First do no harm. Before you start tearing down somebody's PC or installing new software, ask them when they did their last backup, and make sure they understand that they might end up needing it. The most important step in the troubleshooting process is finding out what the problem is, and the best place to start is by asking the customer what's wrong. When dealing with non-technically oriented customers, the next question should always be, what's right, i.e. what works? You'll be surprised how many computers you can troubleshoot over the phone that way.

You need good customers to succeed in business. Good customers buy goods and services you can make an honest profit on and they pay on time. Bad customers, such as those who think you owe them unlimited support because they bought a mouse from you, can ruin you if you don't stand up to them. The natural reaction in all service business is to oil the squeaky wheel, but this often amounts to favoring your bad customers over your good customers. Make sure you take care of the customers who are paying your bills, even if they aren't demanding. Always return phone calls and e-mails, and when you make an appointment, be on time. Don't be afraid to say "I don't know." Just make sure you do know before you see them the next time.

If your business employs more people than just yourself, make sure that everybody knows who should be dealing with customers for what issues. A customer once told me about a salesman who forced a video card into an old-style memory slot while trying to cover service calls. By the same token, you don't want your cracker-jack tech thinking he can quote prices on the spot by adding ten bucks to a price he saw in a magazine. Whether the job at hand is fixing a PC or preparing a complex quote, you and your staff need to finish jobs 100% whenever possible. Procrastination costs you money, customers, and eventually your beauty sleep.

Enjoy Life

The idea of going into business for yourself is not to replace one bad boss with another. Accepting responsibility for your actions is a must, but there's also such a thing as being too hard on yourself. Don't let the job turn into fourteen hour days, seven days a week. If you aren't opening a retail shop, try working out of your home, at least to start. Sure, there are drawbacks, but you'll save a ton of money and there are plenty of benefits as well. If you take yourself too seriously, you'll catch your customers and employees laughing at you behind your back. A small computer business doesn't have much in common with a Fortune 500 company, so don't get caught up play acting. A lack of realistic goals will prevent you from ever winning.

If you aren't happy with what you're doing, odds are your customers and employees aren't really all that happy either. While there's no single cut-and-dry factor that spells the difference between happiness and misery in a financially successful business, keeping it interesting would have to be near the top. For some people, keeping it interesting means never preparing a quote until five minutes before it's due so they can drive like an idiot to get there on time. That sort of challenge is a bit artificial for most of us, who keep it interesting by learning new things and perhaps teaching them as well. Create a website, write a book, develop a new product or add a whole new specialty to your business. If you are too busy to learn something new, it's time to step back and reassess what you're trying to achieve. Just don't forget what pays the bills. As long as you can differentiate between optimism and ignorance, there's no reason to fear new directions.

USEFUL WEB SITES

Computer Business Support Group
  www.groups.yahoo.com/group/computerbusiness

The Service Corps Of Retired Executives (free advice)
  www.score.org

Small Business Administration
(great stuff, and indexes for every state)
  www.sba.gov/starting

IRS site and direct link to 1099 guidelines
  www.irs.gov and www.irs.gov/pub/irs-pdf/p1779.pdf

US business statistics
  www.bizstats.com

Hoover's online for running financial reports business entities
  www.hoovers.telebase.com/form.htm

The Resellers Source Kit (subscription database of suppliers)
  www.rs-kit.com

To check into possible software piracy
  www.bsa.org

National Business Incubation Association
  www.nbia.org/links/index.php .

Co-location for Web Servers
  www.colosource.com/findacolo.asp

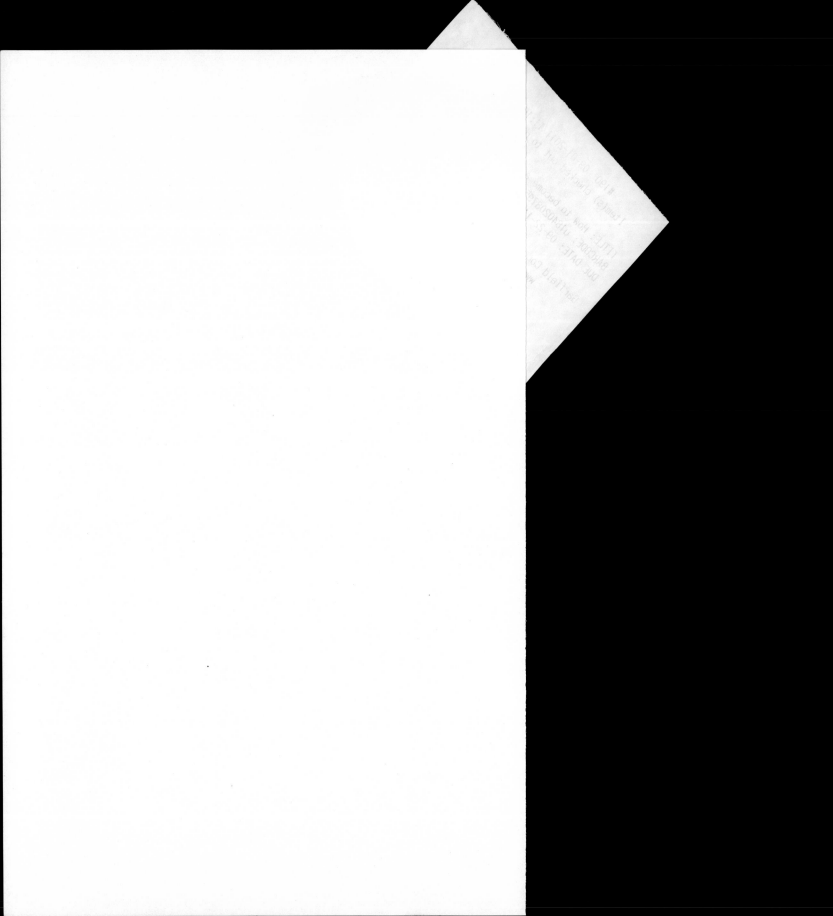

Printed in the United States
37736LVS00003B/120

9 780972 380102